mastering
content creation
and social media
marketing

ARCHITECTURAL INFLUENCE

Thomas Rowntree

RIBA Publishing

Published by RIBA Publishing, 66 Portland Place, London, W1B 1AD

ISBN 978 1 91572 256 0

British Library Cataloguing-in-Publication Data

A catalogue record for this book is available from the British Library.

Commissioning Editor: Alex White
Assistant Editor: Patricia Roig
Production: Marie Doinne
Designed and Typeset by Sara Miranda Icaza
Printed and bound by Pureprint Group Ltd

For product safety concerns and information, please contact our EU representative: Taylor & Francis Verlag GmbH, Kaufingerstraße 24, 80331 Munich, Germany. Email: GPSR@taylorandfrancis.com

www.ribapublishing.com

MIX
Paper | Supporting responsible forestry
FSC® C022913
FSC www.fsc.org

ABOUT THE AUTHOR

Thomas Rowntree, the founder of tomrowstudios, is an architecture social media pioneer as one of the first and largest architecture-focused personal brands on social media. His brand has attracted hundreds of thousands of followers and more than 500,000 monthly views at the time of writing. He has achieved virality, with content reaching millions of views as he shares his message to inspire, educate and guide designers across the globe.

An award-winning architectural designer with a deep passion for both design and media, Thomas explores the multidisciplinary intersections of architecture, communication and branding. Through collaborations with some of the most innovative individuals, brands and products in the architecture space, he has created impactful content that explores the evolving role of social media in the architecture profession. As part of the tomrowstudios ecosystem, Thomas has developed communication courses that equip architecture students and young professionals with the skills to master graphic communication, architectural drawing and portfolio building. His work empowers designers to cultivate their unique creative identity and establish a compelling presence in both the digital and professional spheres.

AN INTRODUCTION TO ARCHITECTURE CONTENT CREATION

Architecture has never been more accessible, thanks to arguably the most powerful visibility tool of our time: **social media**.

The dissemination of architectural knowledge has a long history. Architectural journalism, which emerged with early publications like *Architectural Review* (founded in 1896), was crucial in initiating an alternative education medium by documenting building techniques, materials and styles. These publications sought to set industry standards and provide architects with essential references and inspiration in their practice. The Modernist movement further expanded architectural discourse, with magazines like *Bauhaus* highlighting key Modernist architects and discussing architectural design's social, cultural and political implications, while in the Postmodern era, publications like *Architectural Digest* gained popularity for focusing on visually engaging content that showcased interior design, lifestyle and global architectural trends.

At the time, magazines and architectural journalism emerged as key educational resources for simplifying complex architectural concepts, making them more accessible for architects and beyond. Given that architecture is inherently visual, the synergy between written content and imagery enhanced the communication of architectural ideas, presenting an engaging educational tool.

Fast forward to the 21st century, and while print media has historically shaped architectural discourse and is relevant in the digital age, social media has revolutionised access to architectural knowledge, allowing every corner of the globe to participate in conversations about architecture.

Social media is no longer a novel phenomenon – the first social networking sites emerged in 1997. Today, social media has 4.9 billion active users and an average daily usage of 145 minutes per person.[1] It is a tool that facilitates conversation and connection, breaking down geographic barriers in an instant. It has transformed communication and marketing across every sector. Most notably, industries such as entertainment, retail, fashion, beauty, marketing and real estate fully embrace social media, leveraging its potential to convert audiences into engaged consumers. Social platforms provide anyone with a cost-effective means of expanding their reach, building their network and amplifying their message worldwide.

Despite this, the architecture profession has been slower to capitalise on social media's influence. The question is not whether architects use social media – research from 2024 indicates that 66.7% of UK architectural practices have some form of social media presence[2] – but rather whether they effectively capture attention, engage audiences and build recognition. Collectively, UK architecture firms have a total social media following of 21.2 million across Instagram, LinkedIn, Facebook and X (formerly Twitter). However, this figure is notably low, considering that a single firm, Zaha Hadid Architects, accounts for 14% of those followers at 3 million.

With users' decreasing attention spans and increasing demands for instant gratification, the architecture profession has yet to adapt to the evolving dynamics of social media engagement fully.

While architects have mastered the art of print media, they remain relatively new to the fast-paced world of social media, missing out on a tool that can transform how we connect, build recognition and share our work, knowledge and expertise. In today's digital landscape, your social media presence is now an extension of your CV and portfolio – accessible to future employers, collaborators and audiences worldwide, to you and your business at any scale.

This chapter will explore the many ways in which social media enhances education accessibility and democratises architectural knowledge. It will examine social media's opportunities for increased exposure, professional networking, skill development and entrepreneurship.

ARCHITECTURE AND SOCIAL MEDIA

Undoubtedly, social media has become a powerful tool for many industries; architecture is no exception. It offers immense benefits for individuals and groups at any stage of their careers, from emerging designers and students to established practices. Its accessibility makes it a valuable platform for showcasing work, building brand recognition and engaging with a global audience in ways traditional marketing methods cannot.

Social media will enhance your brand recognition and exposure for architecture practices at any scale. It provides a space to showcase portfolios, highlight existing or future projects, demonstrate expertise, and communicate practice values and services while engaging with an audience and receiving real-time feedback. For emerging designers and students, social media can be used to build a personal brand, gain visibility in a competitive industry and network with industry professionals, helping to gain a competitive edge and build valuable industry relationships. It levels the playing field, offering opportunities for growth and exposure that might otherwise take years to achieve through traditional marketing.

Anyone can explore international projects, gain insights into the work of their favourite designers and practices, and discover new ideas and trends – instantly from their phone or computer. Social media can serve as a travel log for international architecture, documentation of the life of an architect, a digital portfolio, an educational profile and mentorship – giving people a chance to instantly experience, learn and connect with individuals, designs and places across continents.

The accessibility of social media is what makes it so powerful. Anyone can create a profile, share their work and connect with others without needing formal qualifications or a large, if any, budget beyond the resourcing cost; social platforms are free tools. This democratisation of knowledge has broken down traditional barriers in architecture, making it easier for people from all backgrounds to learn, share and access expert advice and guidance. Accessing and sharing architectural expertise no longer requires years of formal education or substantial fees. A social media profile and an internet connection are all you need to share your work, build your network and learn from others.

EDUCATION ACCESSIBILITY

Education is one of the most significant areas of architecture that has benefited most from social media, as its accessibility and fast-paced nature have transformed teaching and learning, providing an engaging, easily accessible learning experience. Social media has become a primary resource for inspiration, education and guidance.

For the architecture profession, the surge in demand for educational content and social media 'guides' and resource profiles has been notable, with many seeking to fill some educational disparities between architecture education and practice. This need for extra learning, and a clearer understanding of the profession, has been around for a long time – it first contributed to the success of architectural magazines in the mid-19th century and now drives the rise of architecture education content creators. In its push for architectural education reform, the Architects Registration Board (ARB) has highlighted significant financial, educational and experience-related barriers within the current system.[3] As a result, students often feel pressured to seek additional learning opportunities. Many turn to social media to upskill and find inspiration, references and precedents, whether architectural drawings, visualisation techniques or insights into diverse architectural styles. How-to guides, tutorials and personal experiences have become key tools for teaching and learning in the digital space. Because of this, architecture content creators have gained popularity, reflecting a growing demand for accessible knowledge and expertise (see Chapter 2: Guide Your Audience).

DEMOCRATISATION

The consequence of social media accessibility for both the consumer and the creator has pushed the democratisation of knowledge and information. It has revolutionised the communication of architectural ideas and education, helping to move the needle against the hierarchical barriers and knowledge gatekeepers, allowing architects and designers of all backgrounds to have a voice, share their work and build their community.

Social media offers anyone from any background, gender and ethnicity the opportunity to share their message, connect with others and fully take ownership of the content they share – all with just the click of the 'publish' button. It offers a space for ownership over your creations and control over the curation of your profile, allowing you to craft your online identity by your means, under your own will. The ownership element may be particularly relevant to the architecture profession when projects typically involve many stakeholders and team members in the delivery of schemes, leaving designers feeling a lack of ownership over their work. Whilst challenges of confidentiality, practice policies of sharing work and company ownership of your work will always remain, social media presents the opportunity to build something with or beyond your day-to-day job under your ownership, under no supervision, with no qualification required. It is an opportunity for individuals to engage with the public on their terms, building a sense of ownership and pride in their work.

The barriers of knowledge, experience and expertise are breaking with social media, changing the landscape of education and ownership. Ultimately, social media has reshaped how we communicate. In a profession as intricate and multifaceted as architecture, these tools are invaluable for fostering a more connected, informed and empowered profession.

WHAT IS ARCHITECTURE CONTENT CREATION?

At this point, you probably have the burning question: What do we define as content creation? Simply put, a content creator produces text, images, audio or video material shared on social media. In the context of architecture, it involves creating content related to the profession to inform, educate or entertain an audience interested in architecture.

Content creation in architecture can include:

+ discussions on different architectural styles
+ sustainable design practices
+ drawing and representation techniques
+ architecture education
+ the promotion of services or completed projects.

As you can imagine, the range of content created is vast, with endless possibilities and avenues to explore.

Content creation varies greatly from creator to business, as each has a unique target audience, niche or brand strategy. For example, one architect might produce blog posts or videos on the design and construction of tiny homes, while another could document their journey of delivering a project, from concept to completion. A practice specialising in sustainable architecture might focus on eco-friendly practices, green materials and sustainable design processes, while an individual architect may offer a behind-the-scenes look at their daily work life and creative process. The purpose of content creation also differs – some aim to educate peers and students, others to attract potential clients or share their passion for architecture with a wider audience.

To give you a little more insight into the types of content found on social media, below are some explanations you can refer to.

It is worth noting that many of these content types are interchangeable and often repurposed; for example, podcasts primarily exist as a long-form type of content but can be broken down into numerous 10-minute, 1-minute or even 10-second pieces of content, providing snippets into short sections of a conversation. Likewise, a live video may later be cut down into three or four 10-minute videos. This is usually intended to tailor the content to each social platform to maximise reach.

Long-Form Video

Long-form video content refers to videos that exceed 5 minutes and offer in-depth coverage of topics. Examples of social platforms like YouTube include documentaries, podcasts, tutorials, vlogs and educational series. People typically consume long-form content to receive more detailed information or insight from the creator.

Short-Form Video

Short-form video content has emerged as the most engaging type of content, capturing the attention of 66% of consumers.[4] As it says on the tin, it is typically brief, lasting anywhere from a few seconds to a few minutes. It is designed to grab the viewer's attention quickly and provide information or entertainment in an easily digestible format. With attention spans dwindling, short-form video content offers a convenient way for users to consume information quickly without exerting much effort. You will find short-form content on social platforms such as TikTok, Instagram reels and YouTube shorts.

Live Video

Live video or streaming involves real-time broadcasting, allowing viewers to watch events as they happen. Examples include YouTube Live and LinkedIn Live, where creators can interact with their audience directly; Twitch, popular for live gaming streams and eSports; and Instagram Live, where influencers and brands can engage followers instantly. People consume live content for its immediacy, authenticity and interactive nature.

Static/images

Photographs, illustrations, infographics and memes are all examples of static/image content. Users on social platforms like Instagram frequently share static/image content to communicate messages visually, capture moments and showcase products. These are often shared as carousels – posts that include more than one image. At the time of writing, Instagram allows up to 20 photos and videos in a carousel.

Blog/Text-Based Posts

Blog and text-based posts are written content shared on WordPress, Medium and LinkedIn platforms. These posts range from articles and essays to personal stories and professional insights. People consume this content for in-depth information, detailed analysis and storytelling.

Audio

Audio content, including podcasts, talks and audiobooks, provides information and entertainment through sound. Podcasts like 'The Diary Of A CEO' on Spotify, talks like TED Talks on Apple Podcasts and audiobooks from Audible offer in-depth listening and convenience.

The main platforms you may find this content on and the focus of this book are:

+ LinkedIn
+ Instagram

+ YouTube
+ TikTok.

LINKEDIN

LinkedIn is a professional social media platform focused on:

+ connections: building professional networks
+ articles: long-form text content sharing
+ posts: updates and professional insights
+ job listings: employment opportunities
+ groups: industry-specific discussions.

LinkedIn is a more professional platform than Instagram or YouTube because it emphasises engagement with industry professionals. LinkedIn facilitates professional growth and networking through direct messages, comments and endorsements, enabling meaningful connections and interactions.

INSTAGRAM

Instagram is a visual social media platform that uses:

+ reels: short-form video content
+ static posts: images and photography
+ stories: 24-hour posts – ephemeral content sharing
+ live: real-time content.

Instagram's visual platform aligns perfectly with architecture's inherently visual nature. Instagram facilitates community building and conversation through direct messages, comments and shares, allowing for direct interaction between creators and consumers. The shareability of visual content makes it a popular choice amongst architecture content creators and brands.

YOUTUBE

YouTube is a video-centric social media platform featuring:

+ videos: long-form video content
+ shorts: short-form vertical (portrait mode) videos
+ live streaming: real-time video broadcasting
+ community posts: text, image and poll posts.

YouTube's video platform is ideal for sharing diverse long and short-form content, from archivisualisation tutorials to documentary-style videos. It facilitates community building and interaction through comments, likes, shares and subscriptions. The platform's recommendation algorithm and search functionality help viewers discover specific video content.

TIKTOK

TikTok is a video-focused social media platform using:

+ TikToks: short-form vertical videos
+ Duets: collaborative video creation.

TikTok's focus on short, engaging videos makes it ideal for capturing attention quickly. The platform encourages community interaction by focusing on shareability and engagement through comments, likes, shares and duets. TikTok's algorithm promotes discoverability, making it easier for content to go viral.

Additionally, you have:

+ X (formerly Twitter)
+ Facebook
+ Snapchat
+ Pinterest.

Architecture, with its inherently visual nature, finds synergy with social media's strengths in engaging visual and verbal communication. Just like architecture is a layered profession that engages multiple senses, the most successful social media profiles use various content types to create a more immersive experience for their audience. Unsurprisingly, the successful architecture profiles have carefully chosen how they create content to communicate their architectural ideas in an engaging and eye-catching way – communicating the visual essence of architecture. They have learned to convey their ideas in easily digestible and engaging formats, captivating audiences and fostering a deeper understanding of their ideas. This book will guide you on how to achieve this yourself.

THE OPPORTUNITY

Architecture is a fiercely competitive profession. Students vie for tutors' approval, graduates seek employment and practices bid for work – it is intense, with everyone looking for an edge. Social media offers that edge.

Building a personal brand, garnering the attention of a global audience and tapping into the 4.9 billion current social media users is a vast opportunity for anyone at any stage of their career and any scale of business. The opportunities on offer are:

+ increased exposure
+ networking
+ upskilling
+ entrepreneurship.

INCREASED EXPOSURE

At a basic level, it's a percentages game; the more your profile is visible, the more your presence is amplified, and the greater your chances are of attracting prospective clients, collaborators and current/future talent.

The viral nature of social media and its innate purpose of global shareability and connectivity make it the perfect tool for gaining exposure. Increased exposure increases the chance of connection, recognition and relationship-building, allowing people to engage, connect, trust and follow your message. It allows you to directly communicate with anyone at any time, enabling you to build a rapport, gather feedback and establish yourself amongst your competitors.

Of course, your appetite for visibility will vary depending on your brand and personal objectives, but being seen is the first step.

NETWORKING

Through increased visibility and presence comes the ability to expand one's network. A core function of social media is to facilitate conversation, and each platform has its unique capacity to communicate and connect in various forms. LinkedIn has connections, Facebook has friends, Instagram has followers, YouTube has subscribers, and all the various shareable, searchable and community tools are available (comments, direct messages, reactions, etc). These tools allow you to connect with individuals and groups in multiple ways – allowing you to manage the depth of your connections and the level of information you share with each – whether through online groups, forums, broadcast channels, etc (see Chapter 3: Brand Influence and Community, to learn about the scalable power of networking and community building).

LinkedIn is most notably the leading platform for professional networking in its ability to facilitate:

+ B2B (Business-to-Business) networking
+ job searching and recruiting
+ professional networking
+ mentorship and coaching
+ industry-specific network groups
+ event and webinar networking.

For professionals in architecture, with its unique competitive nature, connecting with relevant people and building meaningful relationships is critical to open opportunities for employment, collaborations and gaining work. Whether students and graduates want to find their feet in the profession or secure their first work experience, or whether a solo practitioner seeks their next client and collaborator, or practices try to employ new talent, social media's networking capabilities are invaluable.

UPSKILLING

The overlap between architectural skills and those needed for social media branding offers a unique opportunity for cross-disciplinary skill enhancement.

Architecture imparts a diverse array of valuable transferable skills across various creative fields, skills that are valued and excel in content creation and brand building. These skills include visual communication through drawing, diagrams, sketches, presentations, physical and digital models, and visualisation – all of which are communication tools for conveying complex ideas and designs succinctly and effectively. In the competitive world of social media, capturing consumer attention is far more effective with easy-to-understand but eye-catching visual content.

Additionally, verbal communication is another critical skill learned in architecture. We must be confident in our speaking and persuasive conversation to convince and capture the trust of clients, project stakeholders, tutors and colleagues. This demands strong negotiation and interpersonal skills, which are essential for capturing consumers' attention and building relationships with social media audiences. Are you starting to see the parallels?

Constructing a portfolio or Design Access Statement (DAS) in architecture requires fundamental storytelling skills. We learn to build a narrative around the brief, site location, analysis, project constraints, opportunities and design concept through to the final proposal. While the depth of storytelling may vary, the key is to organise visual material and information clearly and concisely to communicate the idea effectively. This ability to craft and present a narrative visually is also a fundamental skill in content creation.

Architecture professionals possess many of the skills required to start creating content. These skills include:

+ visual communication
+ verbal communication
+ sales
+ marketing
+ storytelling.

If you possess any of these skills, you have a major head start.

The opportunity here lies not only in transferring your skills from architecture to content creation, but also in utilising the skills you learn from content creation to upskill and aid your architecture career. They go hand in hand.

Building a social media profile will teach you how to:

+ grab an audience's attention within seconds
+ communicate your ideas succinctly and clearly
+ retain the attention of a viewer
+ connect with a broader audience

+ strategise and create a plan
+ adapt to social and cultural trends
+ collaborate and network
+ monitor data and analyse engagement.

These are all invaluable skills for any individual in any profession.

ENTREPRENEURSHIP

Social media is already a significant sales generator, with 28% of small businesses in the UK relying on it for revenue, and this number is only set to grow.[5] With more exposure, a broader network and refined skills, monetising through social media becomes much easier. The monetary potential for businesses of any size – small, medium, large or global – is massive.

The best part? Beyond resourcing costs, social media is free for anyone to use. For entrepreneurs and individuals, it's an opportunity to showcase products, services or ideas to a global audience, reaching millions of potential customers without the high costs of traditional advertising. You can directly engage with your audience, build relationships and drive sales from a single platform with no cost attached.

There's no denying the immense opportunity social media offers. When used effectively, with the right strategies in place, it can transform how you connect with your audience, build your brand and drive sales. If you leverage its full potential, the benefits will follow.

THE ARCHITECTURAL INFLUENCE STRATEGY

Social media is complex due to its vast range of platforms and content types, constantly changing algorithms, the competitive world of consumer attention and the need for mastering strategy. Navigating this landscape raises a series of questions that may feel familiar to you at this point:

+ What social platforms should I choose?
+ How many platforms should I post on?
+ What content should I create?
+ How much content should I create?

+ How often should I post?
+ How can I monetise my brand?
+ Will this help me grow my business and gain more clients?
+ How can I compete with so many successful social media brands already?
+ Is creating content worth my time?

These questions are the essential starting points for every content creator or business exploring social media marketing. I hope that the last question has been answered.

To help you tackle them, this book serves as a precedent study – an analysis and exploration of the architecture social media landscape, examining successful social media marketing strategies and content creation profiles to offer a blueprint for understanding what works and why it works. This book contains the top architecture-focused personal brands, education profiles, practices and communities that have exploited and benefitted from the opportunity of social media. These profiles have successfully leveraged social media platforms to build global audiences, ranging from 10,000 to 2.5+ million followers at the time of writing.

By presenting these precedents, the book provides a solid foundation – a launchpad for your content creation journey – allowing you to navigate the terrain with a head start. The concept is straightforward: by studying and learning from those who have already excelled, you can adapt and evolve their strategies into something uniquely your own.

In the same way that analysing or studying an architectural precedent is not about replication or copying but rather about stealing and adapting, the goal is to take elements that work and are of interest and modify them to suit your objectives. It's a process of studying what came before and leveraging successful case studies to your advantage, allowing you to build on proven strategies while adapting them to fit your unique message and content strategy.

By studying how content creators and businesses engage with their audiences, communicate their messages, adapt to algorithms and respond to industry trends, you can accelerate your learning curve and discover strategies that aid you with your social media goals.

Engage with this book, study the landscape and discover:

+ Who is currently in the niche?
+ Where is the attention?
+ Where is the money being made?
+ What are others doing in the space?
+ What kind of content is successful in the space?
+ Where there are gaps to exploit (there are currently many)?

Modelling others will help you find relevance and tap into the current and future audiences on the platforms. It will also help you continue to find relevance and to adapt to the ever-evolving social media space. Much like architecture, this process is about evolving your voice and style through ongoing observation, experimentation and refinement. Carving your online profile will be an iterative journey rather than an instant success.

MESSAGE, STRATEGY, PROCESS – THE FRAMEWORK

For the book to successfully analyse existing architecture social media profiles and their strategies, the book will focus on three key features of building your social media brand:

1. Message
2. Strategy
3. Process.

It identifies these three core components for every successful social media profile, and will guide you through each one, breaking them down clearly and systematically. First, you'll understand the profile's message – what it aims to communicate. Second, it will explore the strategy for amplifying that message to reach an audience. Third, it will walk you through creating content designed to amplify that message, making the entire journey easy to follow and apply to your social media efforts.

To make it clear:

1. The **message** is the heart of your brand – it's your identity and the values you stand for. It defines your brand, why it exists and what it aims to communicate. Your message should clearly convey your purpose and goals, making it easy for your audience to understand who you are and what you represent. It's the foundation of your brand, and it should consistently shine through in all the content you create, ensuring that every post, video or image aligns with your core values and resonates with your audience.

2. The **strategy** is about maximising your ability to share your message effectively. Building a strong strategy involves several key elements: choosing the right content types and platforms, defining your target market, identifying your unique selling proposition (USP) and leaning into authenticity. It's also about diversifying your content, telling engaging stories and consistently delivering value. Your strategy will make you stand out, grab consumer attention and sell your services or products. It's the plan that helps you reach your audience, connect with them meaningfully and drive growth for your brand.

3. The **process** is all about how you create your content. It's the practical side of bringing your message and strategy to life. Your message and strategy will shape your content production, influencing everything from the tools you use to the way you present your ideas. Your process could be simple and cost-effective, using just your phone to capture photos and videos, or it could be more elaborate, involving expensive cameras, lights, audio equipment, props or even a dedicated studio space.

By breaking up each profile in this manner, you will gain consistent, detailed insight into their unique message, strategy and process, illustrating successful paths to creating content.

A CONVERSATION WITH
SATWINDER SAMRA

Satwinder Samra is an accomplished architect, inspirational tutor and BAFTA-winning broadcaster. All his work promotes making architecture more accessible.

In a conversation with Satwinder, an experienced architect, teacher, and broadcaster, I was intrigued by his views on social media, given his extensive background in traditional media and television. Satwinder's unique position, encompassing various facets of architecture and exploring the multidisciplinary crossover between architecture practice, education, media and video, provides a rich perspective.

Thomas: *Satwinder, you're an experienced practitioner, tutor and TV presenter. Given your background in architecture, would you encourage students and colleagues to pursue social media and content creation?*

Satwinder: Absolutely. Smart practices are actively engaging with social media. 100%. It helps with reach, awareness and publicity. It also attracts future employees by showcasing a positive work environment. By sharing a practice environment online, future employees can get a vibe about a place. If they can see lots of happy, smiling faces and they're making some models, they go on visits, this looks like a great place to work. Some practices can come over as distant or bland, which can be off-putting.

I often talk to people my age about social media; some don't see its value. I tell them it's essential to show who you are and what it's like to work with you. I've met people and learned things through social media that I wouldn't have otherwise. I engage with social media because I find it relevant.

Thomas: *As someone early in my architecture career, I've noticed much gatekeeping in the field. Students and professionals often hesitate to share their work until it's perfect. Can social media help make architecture more accessible by encouraging people to share their experiences and processes?*

Satwinder: I understand people feel hesitant to share on social media, but making architecture and architectural education more accessible is crucial. The more people engage with architecture, the better. That's my mantra. You're making architecture accessible by sharing, and that's fantastic.

Content creators who share educational and inspirational content create a valuable resource for students and practitioners. It has become an online library of knowledge for individuals seeking guidance. Sharing ideas helps develop them further. I'd definitely produce more content if I had more time and resources. I believe anyone in the creative field should embrace storytelling and sharing. Furthermore, social media lets you share without needing permission. You didn't need a certificate to start; you just did it. I think that is liberating.

Thomas: *It's a huge reason why, in many ways, I pursued social media; I felt like I could. This was something that I had built and something that I had ownership over. This is my work. This is who I am. This is my personality, and I want to express that.*

Satwinder: On the other hand, another thing about creating recorded content is that whatever it is, you can press the 'pause' button. The beauty of the 'pause' button is that you can rewind and watch it again. So, if you're learning or you're trying to understand something better, that's a brilliant thing to be able to do. You can't do that in a live event or a live lecture; you can't press pause and rewind. I also think that's very empowering.

Thomas: *What advice would you give to a sole practitioner or a practice stepping into social media?*

Satwinder: Engage. You can't ignore it. Understand who you are as an organisation and how to communicate that across platforms. I often talk about my work because that's what I know.

Develop your personal brand. Some people in architecture are hesitant about branding, marketing and selling, but if no one knows who you are or what you do, you'll miss opportunities.

01
BUILDING A PERSONAL BRAND

+ A Conversation with Mariana Cabugueira

Success – both professional and personal – often hinges on how effectively you communicate your value to others. Whether sharing your portfolio, bidding to win a competition, applying for a job or selling a product or service, your ability to stand out matters. As you now know, social media offers that edge, but how you define your approach depends on how you want to be seen.

In this chapter, you will learn the leading strategies to foster connection, trust and loyalty with your audience through the curated and strategic approach to personal branding. It will outline how and why personal branding will continue to be one of the most powerful brand strategies.

To unpick the complexities of building a successful personal brand, this chapter will dissect five popular strategies (authenticity, storytelling, brand recognition, unique selling proposition (USP) and niching) and analyse profiles of those who have adopted these strategies to build a successful personal brand.

PERSONAL BRANDING

The term is self-explanatory; a personal brand is a brand that is curated and narrated around you. It is personal to you, as is your message, expertise, experience, values, feelings and attitudes. It is a strategic approach in which you define and express your value through your unique brand. This approach has emerged as one of individuals' and businesses most powerful strategies beyond exposure but also to garner relationships, trust and loyalty, as the brand audience is built upon an emotional connection with an individual and their story.

Corporate branding has long been successful for its ability to capture your attention through colours, imagery, fonts and mission statements, but in today's digital world, where consumers are increasingly drawn to the people and personalities behind the brand, it is authenticity, reliability and human connection that truly build trust and loyalty. While corporate branding focuses on the company as a whole – its products, services and values – which can feel distant and impersonal, personal branding emphasises personal stories, values and experiences to create a deeper, more emotional, connection with an audience; personal branding is stealing the limelight.

The beauty and challenge which comes with building a personal brand is that your brand is about you, and so the constant battle is to embrace your unique self, with all its imperfections, and garner the courage to share that with the world. While you have control over the curation of your brand image, where you determine what you do and don't share, the many successful personal brands have shown their vulnerabilities and consequently built the human connection that comes with honesty and authenticity.

It requires you to be vulnerable, reflective and critical. Inevitably, with increased visibility, people will have things to say, whether positive or negative. Opening up and sharing yourself with the world requires courage and conviction. To quote the founder of Amazon, Jeff Bezos, 'Your brand is what other people say about you when you're not in the room.'

The next challenge is that whilst this book will outline successful strategies to increase exposure and connection with your brand, there is no specific strategy or approach that is right or wrong. It comes down to the story you want to tell and owning it; presenting it through your unique lens. This 'freedom' allows you to be flexible and follow your interests. It evolves with you, adapting to new experiences, skills and insights gained over time. For instance, someone passionate about architectural drawing might start by sharing their drawings and the process behind creating them, but as they grow, they might also incorporate their journey of visiting world-renowned architecture, drawing as they travel and hosting workshops teaching individuals how to learn their drawing style. While the core identity and messaging of the brand remain, the content evolves with the individual, keeping the personal brand dynamic and engaging.

Personal branding is more complex than mere self-promotion; it's about curating a brand that is authentic to you, your skillset, your knowledge and expertise. It's not about showing off what you have and what you have achieved, but providing real value to others, whether by offering guidance, entertainment or insights.

Approaches to Authentic Content

The most common approach to building a personal brand is through documentation – the act of recording and sharing an individual, brand or organisation through the journey. That journey may be an architectural project from start to finish, a drawing process, behind-the-scenes of life in practice, the curation of a portfolio or a construction sequence on site. This 'show, not tell' approach is successful because it is grounded in sharing value, whether educational and insightful or for entertainment.

This approach has authenticity at its core, as the process of documenting is unique to each individual or practice, making it a rewarding proposition for solo practitioners and practices at any scale. You may decide to build a brand through the documentation of your:

+ **Work:** Sharing your unique process, design and construction methods or practice values will make your brand authentic. Giving insights into your methods will affirm expertise and build credibility.
+ **Knowledge and experience:** Positioning yourself as a guide to share your knowledge and experience through your journey will foster connection. The individual establishes loyalty and trust with their audience by providing insights, lessons learned and expertise.
+ **Lifestyle:** Documenting one's journey through life and unique processes offers a personal and relatable touch to a personal brand. This approach involves sharing personal stories, challenges and achievements, giving the audience a glimpse into the individual's daily life and the highs and lows of their journey.

ABBY.ARCHITECTURE

Abby Happel is a junior architect and social media content creator with a Master of Architecture from UC Berkeley (University of California, Berkley) and a Bachelor of Environmental Design in Architecture from NC State (North Carolina State University).

SOCIAL PLATFORMS

+ TIKTOK
  @abbyhappel
+ INSTAGRAM
  @abby.architecture

CONTENT TYPES

+ Short-form video
  (7–20 seconds)
+ Image carousels

MESSAGE

The abby.architecture profile captures the essence of authenticity by documenting her journey through architecture. Abby's brand identity tells the story of her day-to-day life in architecture and the trials and tribulations of training to become an architect. She shares a realistic and relatable perspective on what it's like to be in the profession.

Abby started her personal brand by posting her work to TikTok during her bachelor's degree at NC State. Soon after, her projects gained popularity, attracting other architecture students and creatives interested in her work process.

She shares, 'I recognised the lack of architecture students and professionals sharing their experiences online. From my time in architecture school to embarking on my experience in practice, I've documented successes and uncertainties as I navigate this journey. I feel that this transparency has resonated with others... I'm not hesitant to showcase my struggles because they are an integral part of the journey, just as much as everything else.'

STRATEGY

Abby's primary social media strategy revolves around exploring and documenting her architectural projects and lifestyle, leaning into a young audience and establishing herself as a recognised figure in this niche. She has successfully built an audience that appreciates her authenticity by tapping into the demand for genuine and relatable architecture documentation content through fast-paced, short-form content.

Through documenting her journey, Abby has gained followers who witness her career's real-time progression and evolution, creating a narrative that her followers can follow and invest in. This shared journey becomes a powerful connection point, as fellow students at similar career stages can relate to the shared experiences. Whether it's the stress of a portfolio submission, the excitement of a design breakthrough or the camaraderie of studio life, these moments are universal experiences for those in architecture education. While her primary strategy is to focus on the architecture documentation niche, Abby further differentiates herself by pursuing other methods that make her unique.

Figure 1.1 Abby with a UC Berkeley classmate.

Figure 1.2 Abby graduating from UC Berkeley.

Humour

Humour plays a pivotal role in Abby's content, providing relief and a sense of solidarity for students overwhelmed by the rigours of their studies. She leverages comedy to build an emotional connection and camaraderie among architecture students who face the demanding nature of the field. Abby's content brilliantly incorporates humour and relatability, making architecture students and professionals feel seen. A key example is her point of view (POV)-style reels, which playfully exaggerate everyday struggles in architecture school. One example reel, 'POV: That One Toxic Person in Your Architecture Studio', pokes fun at students' sleep-deprived, overworked reality. Her humour extends to architecture software struggles, jokingly preferring *Minecraft* for modelling or highlighting how she spent an entire episode of *Love Is Blind* working on a single-section drawing.

Figure 1.3 Abby documenting her thesis precedent: Nakagin Capsule in Tokyo.

Figure 1.4 The 'Frame Flux' project model by Abby Happel and Fulin Huang.

Abby explains, 'In architecture education and practice, the demanding nature of the field fosters camaraderie among those who understand its challenges and can find humour in them.' Through playful, self-aware content, she creates a space where architects and students can laugh at their shared experiences, making her content both engaging and deeply relatable.

This strengthens her bond with fellow architecture students and broadens her appeal to wider audiences. Abby says, 'I've noticed that my content often reaches those outside of the field, as they're intrigued by the stark differences between my day-to-day life from other educational paths (even my friends outside of the program do not fully understand what is going on during the long hours spent in the studio, hidden away on campus).'

Figures 1.5–1.6 Stills from an Abby's short-form content.

Trending Content

In addition to humour, Abby integrates current Instagram and TikTok trends into her content. She utilises trends in two forms:

1. **Trending sounds**
   She aligns her edits with trending sounds or popular music – these can be found on the trending sound libraries on social platforms.

2. **Popular trends**
   She leans into popular and relevant topics with her content.

By leaning into trends, she aligns herself with current interests and sounds, increasing the likelihood of your posts being seen and shared by social media algorithms. This approach allows

Figure 1.7 The 'Frame Flux' project model by Abby Happel and Fulin Huang.

Figure 1.8 Abby's thesis project 'Metabolizing Metabolism', based in Tokyo.

her to diversify her audience and extend her reach to a broader design audience who enjoy trending content. Abby ensures her content stays relevant and engaging by tapping into popular trends. While she finds this an effective strategy, she emphasises that 'connecting your niche to broader trends is often simpler for quick engagement than creating entirely new formats and content from scratch. However, relying solely on this approach has its limitations. Maintaining a sense of originality is crucial for developing a compelling personal brand. Therefore, I advise you always to pioneer some of your content ideas.'

Figure 1.9 Abby's 'Urban Agricultural Utopia' project rendering.

Architectural Skill

Abby's content is not just about lifestyle. She also creates incredible architectural drawings and visualisations that people appreciate. These works serve as both a source of inspiration and a reference point for others. Abby's high skill level makes her work stand out; she has a simple, clean but professional communication style with her drawings, renders and models – skills that are admirable as an architecture student. Her audience recognises and values this skill, as some of her most engaged posts have been her architectural pieces. This highlights how much people are captivated by her ability to create such impressive work. They're eager to see more of her projects and are particularly interested in the behind-the-scenes process that brings her creations to life.

Figure 1.10 Abby in the studio.

PROCESS

Abby's production process is remarkably simple. She films everything using her phone, capturing raw and genuine moments while ensuring high video quality. Editing is done using CapCut, a free app that lets her quickly stitch together clips on her phone. She explains, 'I don't even use a stand for my phone; I usually just prop it against my water bottle. You don't necessarily need costly equipment or extensive editing skills to thrive on social media. I also rarely have content ideas ahead of time; I just organically post when the ideas come to me.'

This simple approach contributes to her authenticity, amplifying her content's personal and relatable feel. Her minimalist technique underscores a sense of honesty and accessibility. Her videos' intimate, diary-like nature reflects a real and unpolished glimpse into her life, emphasising her brand message.

Figure 1.11 Abby's video editing process in CapCut.

Figure 1.12 Abby in the studio.

STORYTELLING

Storytelling is a compelling strategy due to the intrinsic human affinity for stories. The power of stories lies in their ability to captivate and engage audiences, holding their attention far more effectively than mere facts or typical advertisements. Think about how movies work – they immerse us in characters' lives and take us through emotional journeys, often keeping us hooked for hours. Movies are captivating because they explore universal themes like love, struggle, triumph, hope and personal growth, which we all can relate to on some level. Whether it's a story of redemption or a fantasy tale, these narratives stay with us, making the experience more memorable and even fostering loyalty to the characters or the story.

The same principles can be applied to building your personal brand. Take Abby as an example. She shares her journey through a relatable lens, showing the highs and lows of architecture school; a storytelling tactic that works because her stories are authentic. When a personal brand tells a story, it engages people deeper, making them want to connect and participate. If a brand shares a story of overcoming obstacles, it can strike a chord with someone going through a similar challenge. This kind of connection is far more powerful than traditional marketing because it's not just transactional; it's emotional.

The emotional connection is key. When a brand makes people feel something, they're more likely to remember it. And at the end of the day, building a brand is all about being memorable.

Austin Kleon, in his book *Show Your Work! 10 Ways to Share Your Creativity and Get Discovered*, emphasises that storytelling is a key element in building a strong personal brand. He explains, 'If you want to be more effective when sharing yourself and your work, you need to become a better storyteller. You need to know what a good story is and how to tell one.'[1]

INITIATE ARCHITECTURE (ROSS HARTLAND)

Ross Hartland founded Bridgend-based practice Initiate Architecture, a solo studio dedicated to bringing new life, light and joy to old buildings.

SOCIAL PLATFORMS

+ INSTAGRAM @initiatearchitecture
+ YOUTUBE @initiatearchitecture
+ TIKTOK @initiatearchitecture

CONTENT TYPES

+ Short-form video (7–20 seconds)
+ Long-form video (5–20 minutes)
+ Image carousels
+ Text graphics

MESSAGE

Initiate Architecture is a profile run by Ross Hartland, who documents and shares his story: 'My story began with unhappiness in corporate practice where, despite enjoying the projects and relationships, I struggled with the realities of the profession. Like many others, I experienced a low salary for high responsibility, unpaid overtime, long commutes and rigid work hours.'

After seven years of education and several years of practice experience, Ross was disappointed with the corporate reality. He began saving a portion of his corporate salary as a financial runway to support the launch of his own studio, hoping he could design a business that would bring the creative freedom, flexibility and financial reward he was missing.

He states, 'As a young architect, I had heaps of passion, but natural apprehension and imposter syndrome were exacerbated by navigating the technicalities of managing a design studio through trial and error. It was clear that architects did not communicate their experiences transparently, especially concerning fees and financial matters.'

Recognising this, Ross consciously focused his social media message on authentic lessons and insights gained from his own experiences – learning and sharing as he went – hoping that it would guide other architects on their entrepreneurial journeys. He explains, 'My aim was twofold: to provide valuable resources for those facing similar challenges and to encourage a culture of openness among architect peers by sharing the good and not-so-good reality.'

Initiate's content became designed to communicate behind the scenes of his architectural work as a sole practitioner – aimed at informing prospective clients of the value of his process and service – alongside information that would have helped him understand simple rules of business, practice management and process that aren't always covered in architecture school.

STRATEGY

Ross is unique in that he is one of the only solo practitioners actively building an online profile by documenting his journey and sharing the trials and tribulations openly. This approach may be described as 'becoming a large fish in a small

Figure 1.13 Initiate's studio following an 'architecture coffee morning'.

Figure 1.14 Recording a sketching session.

pond' and it allows his brand to stand out in a less crowded space, establishing a strong and recognisable presence. His transparency about the challenges, triumphs and processes as a solo practitioner resonates with a specific audience interested in pursuing a solo career themselves.

Ross explains, 'My content evolved into a creative record of the weekly activities, thoughts and lessons learned. Surprisingly, this insight proved equally fascinating to clients, architects, designers and students. By communicating transparently about design, money and business, my audience grew steadily with interested people who relate to my successes and challenges. Architects, designers and students were particularly engaged in the day-to-day realities of solo practice – a journey they were perhaps planning to follow – while prospective clients valued the openness.'

Figure 1.15 Documenting site visits.

Figure 1.16 Showcasing life in the studio.

By candidly telling his story, Ross provides valuable insights and lessons rarely discussed openly in the industry. He delves into subjects like:

+ navigating budgets
+ fee calculations
+ planning constraints
+ break-even rates
+ intricacies of Building Regulations submissions.

He openly discusses these critical processes by documenting his solo practice, offering fellow and aspiring solo practitioners' guidance and precedent. Ross's transparency helps demystify the complexities of the design and build process, empowering others in the field to navigate their projects with greater understanding and confidence.

Figure 1.17 Documenting a condition survey in a vacant chapel.

Education, Inspiration and Promotion

Initiate Architecture content is primarily published on Instagram as short-form videos and carousels. Ross finds this a successful approach to document his journey and explain his work processes visually. He describes his approach to creating content as organic and authentic, responding to lessons, thoughts and experiences he encounters in the studio that he wishes to share. He also has a strategy to create content around the following three core pillars:

1. Education (50%)

The how to do something or 'how I do something' pillar is about giving away great value for free, intended to help others and grow an audience. It often achieves the most organic reach and indirectly promotes Initiate's architectural services and digital product offerings to clients, architects and designers.

Figure 1.18 Ross presenting the opportunities, lessons and challenges of solo practice.

Figure 1.19 Recording the process of making models.

2. Inspiration (30%)

The 'what does the life of an architect look like' pillar is essential to Ross because it shows his life and identity as a professional architect who does not solely focus on project work. Unveiling his life in the studio helps him to build trust and a personal connection with his clients and audience; for example, a day in my life, a morning in the studio, etc.

3. Promotion (20%)

Ross explains that the 'promotion' pillar, including direct promotional content is important, but this only equates to 20% of his posts. Instead of repetitively selling, he aims to give away huge value for free through the two previous content pillars, which will buy you the right to promote directly occasionally.

Figure 1.20 Ross illustrating his thinking and design process.

Figure 1.21 Ross recording his work in real time.

PROCESS

Ross's production quality is high, with attention to detail in colour, lighting, composition and typography. Such a level of production demonstrates professionalism and quality within his content.

Much of his content production surrounds his solo architecture studio routine. Ross explains, 'My typical day follows this methodology whenever possible, dividing my time into a morning of "making" from 07:00 to 12:00 and an afternoon of "managing" from 13:00 to 16:00. The making phase consists of drawing, drafting, designing, model making, visualising, filming and editing – exclusively focused on creative work when I feel most energised. In the afternoon, the managing phase involves handling emails, meetings, business development, phone calls, invoicing and other administrative tasks. Considering solely the time required to film,

Figure 1.22 Sharing behind the scenes of drawing production and practices.

Figure 1.23 Ross talking to a camera in his studio.

edit and publish content within the company, it consumes an average of one day of my working week.'

Ross's production process typically follows these steps, which can be adapted for your own needs and style:

1. Ideation – Notion template

Ross intentionally documents ideas in reaction to real-life challenges, reflections or successes that arise whilst running his studio. Documenting these ideas allows him to respond to them immediately or revisit them. He states, 'These ideas need to be recorded and scheduled, so I use a Notion template to capture the format (long-form, short-form or carousel), the platform (Instagram, TikTok, YouTube), the intended publication date and presentation details (look and feel, language and tone).'

2. Filming – practicality

The filming of these ideas is, as far as practically possible, captured in real time. You can build habits such as setting up a camera to record a sketching or model-making session, taking a camera to the site or screen recording a visualisation tutorial as it's happening. This is an essential skill as there isn't the time to re-produce work solely for video content.

3. Post-production – Adobe Premiere Pro

Once the footage is captured, Ross dedicates half a day per week, typically on a Friday afternoon, to editing videos in Adobe Premiere Pro or creating carousels in Adobe Photoshop. When project work doesn't get in the way, he maintains a schedule of two posts per week on Instagram and TikTok, and one per month on YouTube.

CHRIS SIMMONS

An experienced architect, illustrator and educator, Chris Simmons is the founder of the mentoring platform Architects Instruction, supporting architects with their careers.

SOCIAL PLATFORMS

+ LINKEDIN
  Chris Simmons
+ INSTAGRAM
  @chrissimmons0

CONTENT TYPES

+ Short-form video (30–60 seconds)
+ Image carousels
+ Text graphics

MESSAGE

Chris shares insights into his knowledge and experience as an architect, associate partner, tutor and visiting critic. He shares a message of positivity about the profession and how people can achieve happy, healthy and well-paid careers, explaining, 'I have benefitted from the support of key mentors during my career. I want to promote the benefits of mentorship within the industry, combating the negativity around the profession online with actionable career advice and support. I aim for my personal brand and that of "Architects Instruction" to imbue positivity and creativity, providing a nurturing environment to grow. I like to position myself as "old enough to be experienced yet young enough to be relevant".'

Chris has been a qualified architect for a decade and uses his own experiences from a career in a large London architecture practice as his content pillars. Most people succeeding with social media in architecture are students documenting their way through university into qualification. He explains, 'This has much merit for an audience but not the lived experience for people further into their careers, which is where I come in. I am an authentic voice with experience and want to help the next generation.'

STRATEGY

Chris stands out in this landscape as an experienced architect and associate partner, an intentional move on his behalf to offer a depth of knowledge and a level of authority that few on the platform share. By sharing his expertise and engaging with topics that matter, Chris builds authority and attracts an audience eager for guidance from a seasoned professional.

Communication, Negotiation and Leadership

To communicate his message, Chris focuses on three key soft skills with his content:

1. Communication
2. Negotiation
3. Leadership.

Much of Chris's content is short-form reels in which he speaks in a relaxed setting and straight to the camera to offer a conversational feel. This is an effective approach, as it makes the audience feel they are being spoken to directly and can easily engage with the information provided. He shares, 'Video is a great opportunity to create engaging content and build rapport

Figure 1.24 Chris's social media profile image with his signature yellow.

Figure 1.25 Chris sketching in the office.

with your intended customers. If you are consistent, people will get to know, like and trust you over time.'

While he shares his depth of knowledge and experience in architecture, Chris also posts about personal moments with his family and daily activities. He highlights his communication, negotiation and leadership skills and emphasises his roles as a dad, husband and architect. By occasionally sharing images of his son, wife, younger self and everyday life, Chris provides a holistic view of his world, making his audience feel more connected to his profile.

Architects Instruction Branding

Chris's profile features his mentoring platform 'Architects Instruction', which he describes as having a 'positive and nurturing message, guiding you on your journey through

Figure 1.26 An example of Chris's infographic posts highlighting his roles.

Figure 1.27 An example of Chris's video content.

architecture, whatever path you take'. The platform offers career coaching, personal branding guidance, project and presentation reviews, and more.

The Architects Instructions brand is well integrated into Chris's profile, with clear and consistent branding that makes his profile recognisable and memorable.

His social media profile stands out through consistent and clear messaging, embodying his happy and positive learning philosophy. This message is encapsulated in his bright, playful and sketchy branding. Two distinct features contribute significantly to making Chris' profile recognisable and memorable: his use of bright yellow and his sketchy theme.

Figure 1.28 Chris's sketch of Portland Head Lighthouse, Cape Elizabeth, Maine, USA.

Figure 1.29 Chris's sketch of the ruin of Calda House, Lairg, Scotland.

1. Colour – bold yellow

Chris employs a consistent colour scheme of yellow, white and black throughout his profile and content. Yellow, a bold and attention-grabbing colour, dominates his social media presence, making his posts instantly recognisable. This vibrant hue appears prominently on his profile grid, in the background of his photos, on his yellow table and in the yellow tracing paper and sticky notes he uses. The consistent application of yellow creates a cohesive visual experience, ensuring that his content stands out in a crowded social media feed and evokes warmth and positivity.

2. Sketchy theme

Chris incorporates a sketchy theme. By leaning into the key communication tool of an architect – drawing – Chris integrates a sketchy tone into his posts and signifies creativity and

Figure 1.30–1.31 Examples of Chris's infographic posts highlighting advice to architects.

hands-on processes related to architecture. This approach underscores his brand identity and promotes an engaging and dynamic learning experience. The stills in Figures 1.30 and 1.31 demonstrate how Chris consistently integrates his signature yellow to create a cohesive, recognisable brand identity.

PROCESS

Like Sketching

Chris describes his production as sketching in architecture, and explains, 'The most creative part of the process is the ideation and writing. During this phase, you are researching, reflecting and testing out ideas. It is the most time-consuming element of the process but also the most enjoyable. I pick up and put down scripts for videos and have a simple Notion template to store them in to keep organised.'

Figure 1.32 Chris's content ideation dashboard in Notion.

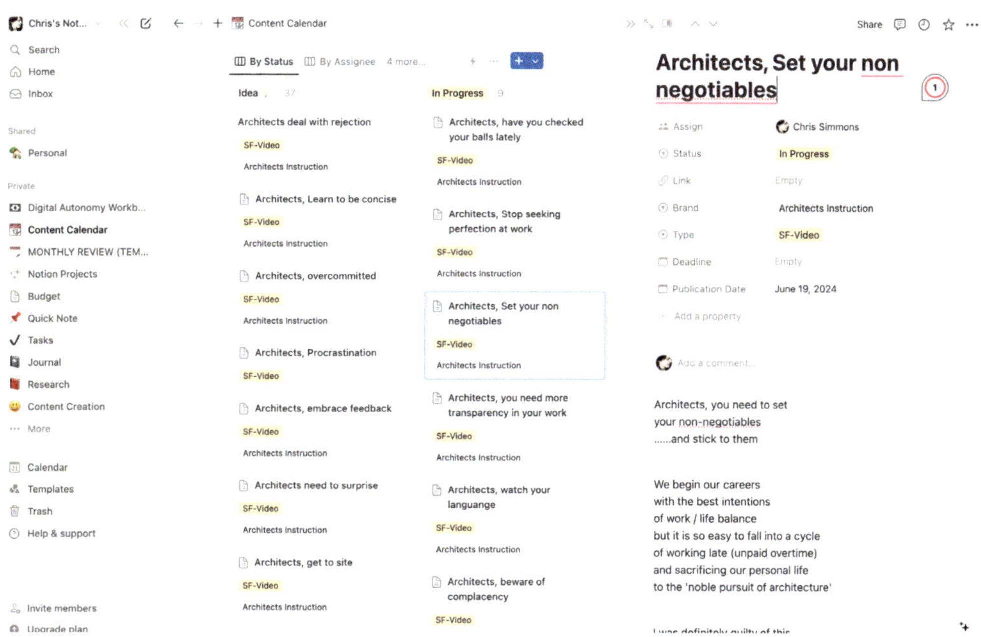

High-Quality Production

While Chris approaches his content conversationally, he emphasises that high-quality production is critical to his content strategy, explaining, 'Most creators will tell you to start filming videos with whatever device you have. I didn't listen. I spent a long time amassing professional-level equipment and learning production techniques before I filmed one video. I aspired for my content to have a quality edge, and whilst I think quality is an important factor in my growth, I don't want it to stand as a barrier for people to get started with social media.'

Batch Production

Chris typically films in batches, as it takes time to set up the equipment, typically 10 videos over a session. He then edits the videos in chunks, always considering the speed and flow of the videos and how this information will be absorbed in short form.

Figure 1.33 Chris's filming set-up with camera, lighting and script.

Figure 1.34 Chris presenting a workshop for young architects.

BRAND RECOGNITION

The essence of branding is creating simple, relevant messages that we repeat time and again to become part of the public consciousness. This repetition not only helps the brand to become memorable but it also helps your audience to form an expectation of what content to anticipate, ensuring they are more likely to follow and engage. Conversely, if your content and approach vary widely, it can confuse your audience, leading to a lack of engaging viewers and people willing to follow your profile. Clarity is crucial. People are drawn to profiles that provide clear, specific, consistent value.

For instance, companies like Apple, Adidas and McDonald's have established powerful brands by consistently using colours, logos, messaging and identity:

+ Apple's clean, minimalist design, consistent packaging and branding, and innovative message constantly highlight simplicity and innovation.
+ Adidas's consistent and strategic use of its iconic three stripes is distinctive and symbolises quality, performance and style, making it instantly recognisable.
+ McDonald's golden arches and consistent colour scheme make it the most recognisable brand globally. This branding evokes reliability and convenience.

In these examples, consistency and repetition drive home the brand's message through every product, product packaging, advertisement, store design, layout and experience. These elements and consistency make their brands instantly recognisable and memorable, creating a lasting impression on consumers. While your brand is on a much smaller scale and focused on social media content, the same principles apply.

ACTIONABLE STEP

To build brand recognition, focus on three key aspects:

1. **Consistency**
   Ensure that your visual elements, messaging and overall style are uniform across your content and branding. This includes your colour palette, logo, fonts, and content's production quality, tone and style. Consistency helps reinforce your brand identity, making it easier for your audience to remember and recognise you.

2. **Style**
   Develop a unique style that sets you apart. This could be your filming or editing technique, music genre, how you talk, the tone of your message or how you frame and capture your video content. A distinctive style makes your content more appealing and strengthens brand identity.

3. **Value**
   Offer content that provides value to your audience. Whether it's educational, entertaining or inspirational, ensure your content meets the needs and interests of your target audience. Valuable content encourages engagement, fosters loyalty and makes your audience more likely to return.

By focusing on consistency, style and value, you can build a strong, recognisable brand that stands out on social media and encourages returning viewers.

TOMROWSTUDIOS

Thomas Rowntree, founder of tomrowstudios, documents his journey as an architectural designer, providing insightful knowledge and experience to architecture students and professionals.

SOCIAL PLATFORMS

+ INSTAGRAM @tomrowstudios
+ YOUTUBE @thomasrowntree
+ LINKEDIN Thomas Rowntree

CONTENT TYPES

+ Short-form video (5–60 seconds)
+ Long-form video (2–30 minutes)
+ Image carousels
+ Text-based carousels

Before analysing my social media profile, it's helpful to give you some context about my journey. I started creating content in 2017 when I was 17, pursuing a social media career in fitness and bodybuilding. At the time, I was incredibly passionate about everything related to fitness – training, nutrition, sleep, routines – anything to maximise my gym performance. I followed fitness YouTubers who vlogged their daily lives, showing what they ate, how they trained and their fitness-focused routines. These creators garnered high viewership and gained brand sponsorships, sold their products and built successful businesses – all from making YouTube videos. I was fascinated by their lifestyle and the creative process behind it, so I decided to give it a shot.

Before creating my first YouTube video, I had never filmed or edited before. I had some photography knowledge, but video was new territory. I filmed, chopped up the clips, picked a favourite song and compiled a short montage for my first upload. From that moment, I developed a love for documenting. I began documenting my life, primarily focusing on fitness and eventually settled into a consistent routine of posting two videos a week by the time I turned 18. I studied the fitness creators I admired – how they filmed, spoke to the camera, framed their shots, chose music and edited their videos. I even paid attention to their posting schedules, video titles and thumbnails. I modelled my content after theirs on a small scale and, initially, it worked; I hit 1,000 subscribers in my first year, and one of my videos surpassed 20,000 views.

Amidst this, I started architecture school, and it consumed me. I hadn't fully researched what I was getting into and there wasn't much online showing what architecture school was like. Coming from a background of watching fitness creators document their journeys, I was shocked to see that no one in the architecture field seemed to be doing the same. There were no vlogs or behind-the-scenes content giving insight into studying architecture, dealing with deadlines or balancing life as a student.

A few months into school, with architecture submissions taking over my schedule and reducing my gym time, I decided to film a day in the life of an architecture student. It was a shot in the dark, something I hadn't seen before in the architecture space. To my surprise, the video performed exceptionally well; it reached 30,000 views in its first month and is now my most-watched video on YouTube, with over 228,000 views.

Figure 1.35 Thomas's 'Trans[port] Masters of Architecture' project.

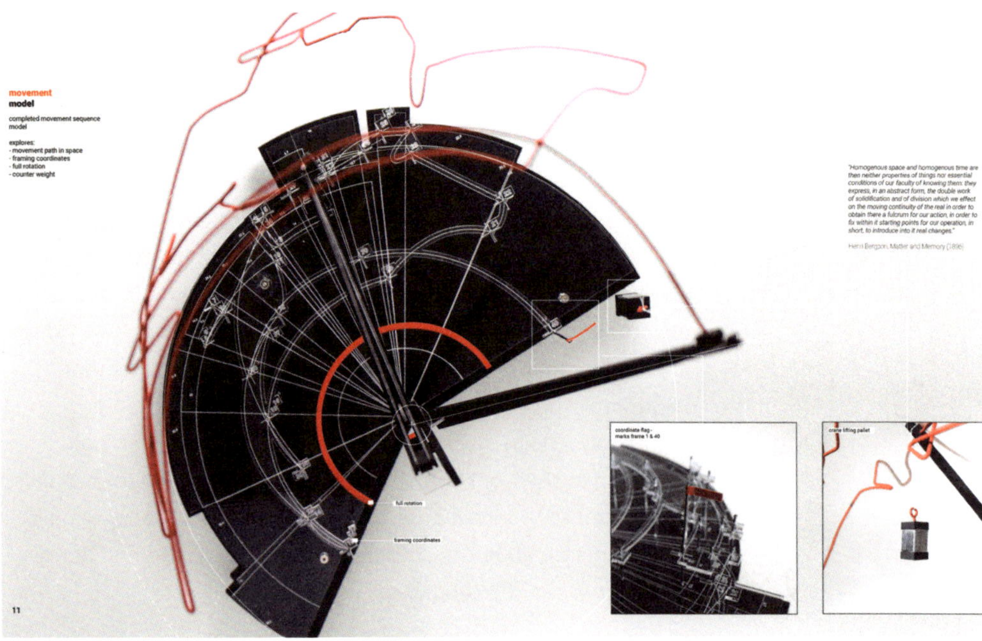

I had tapped into something. People were eager to see what architecture school was like from a student's perspective. My content offered a behind-the-scenes look into portfolio building, model making, drawing, and how I managed my time and submissions while balancing gym life and creating YouTube videos. This began my journey as an architecture content creator.

MESSAGE

tomrowstudios still embodies the same core message and identity that it began with – it's about me, my journey and my intention to share my lessons and learnings to help others on their path. The message is clear: I am an architectural designer navigating my career in architecture, and I want to share my experiences to help you. With the focus on documentation, the brand also reflects my interests, ambitions, the content I enjoy and how I wish to be seen by others – in many ways, it is a digital

Figure 1.36 Thomas's 'Trans[port] Masters of Architecture' project.

portfolio of me, my work and my personality. Some of the core values that I share are:

+ creativity
+ expression
+ exploration
+ balance – well-being.

These values are communicated consistently in every aspect of my content, from how I film and edit to the tone of my videos, how I speak to the camera, the captions I write and the look and feel of my pages. While the brand has a strong foundation in the architecture niche, I still see it as something personal.

Figure 1.37–1.38 Examples of Thomas's video content.

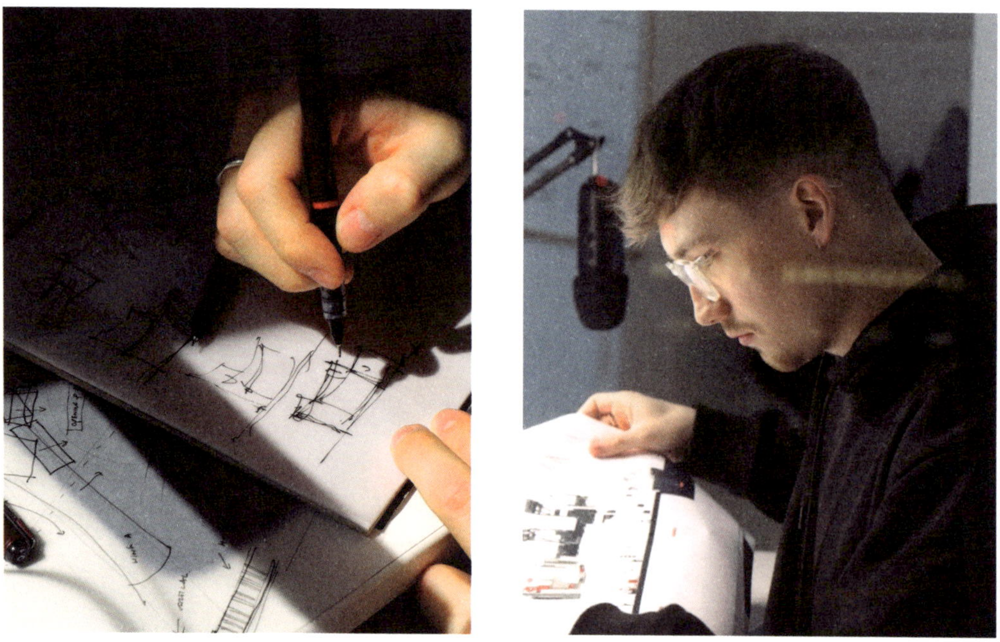

STRATEGY

Identity and style are fundamental to the tomrowstudios brand. From the aesthetic tone of my videography, editing and lighting to my architectural design and communication style, I strive to portray visual excellence across all platforms.

1. Stylistic content

As I document my career in architecture, I've shared my architectural drawings, portfolios, sketches, models and nearly every aspect of my project development. This transparency has sparked interest in my work and attracted an audience that resonates with it. My designs, influenced by figures like Zaha Hadid, Enric Miralles and Daniel Libeskind, lean towards expressive geometries, often exploring overlapping forms, shapes, harsh edges and bold contrasts – a style that could be described as abstract.

Figure 1.39–1.40 Examples of Thomas's video content.

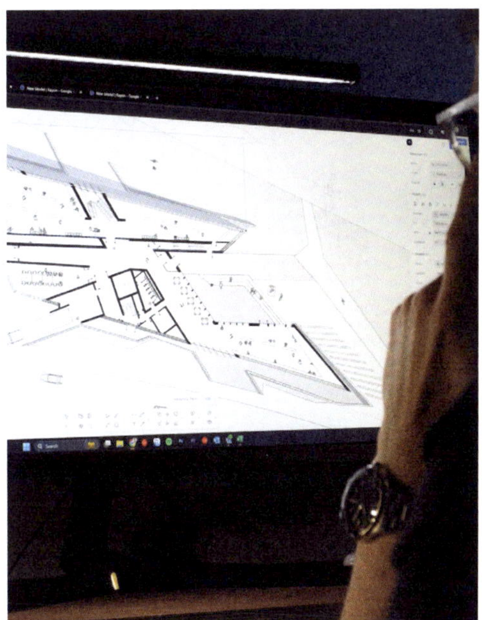

Similarly, my communication style reflects this boldness. My architectural drawings feature strong contrasts, bold colours and intricate linework. I've consistently applied this aesthetic, which has helped me build a recognisable identity throughout my architectural work.

While unconventional, these design choices push boundaries, making my work distinctive and helping them stand out. I have also found this true through sharing my work on social media; my architectural style has become a feature of the content that people can recognise and associate with me and my brand.

In addition to my architecture, my videography and photography are equally carefully crafted. I'm passionate about cinematography and storytelling, using elements like colour grading, lighting, framing, editing rhythm and audio to create

Figure 1.41 An example of Thomas's video content, giving advice.

content with high production value. My videos are intentionally cinematic and aesthetically pleasing, designed to grab attention for their visual appeal and story. I focus on creating aesthetic but meaningful content, which has become a key part of my online presence. The images in Figures 1.37-1.40 showcase the visual style of video content featured on the tomrowstudios page.

2. Value through content diversification

I seek to provide value in many forms. Across tomrowstudios platforms you'll find:

+ highly produced short-form videos (5–15 seconds)
+ short videos where I speak directly to the camera, offering advice or insights (30–60 seconds) – I call these 'speaking reels'
+ long-form video content on YouTube – drawing breakdowns, studying tips or lifestyle advice

Figure 1.42 Thomas's YouTube channel.

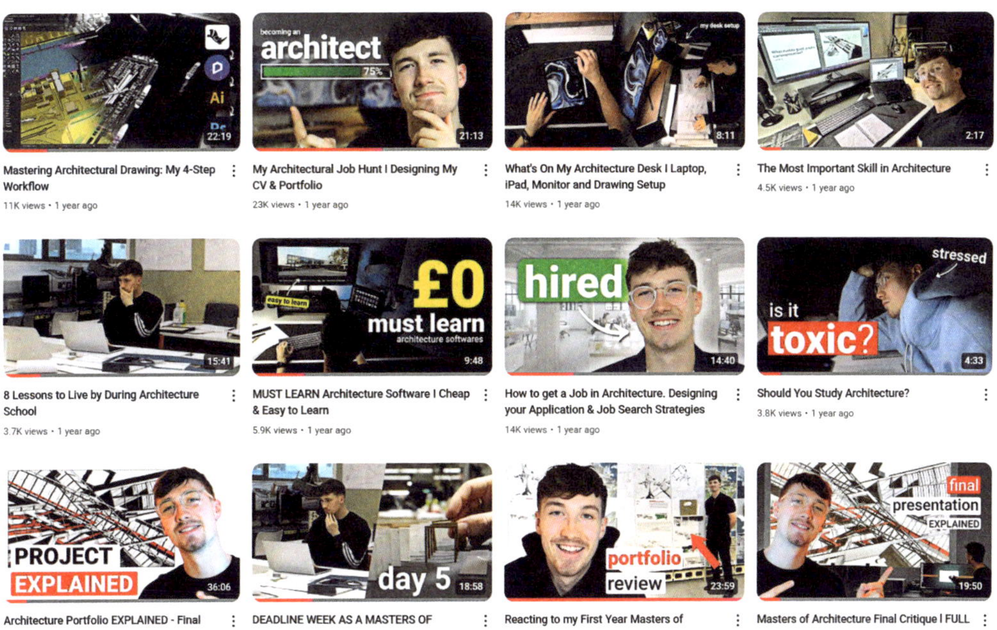

+ vlogs that give a behind-the-scenes look into my daily life
+ image carousels showcasing my life as a designer, along with day-to-day activities – which I call 'archi dump'
+ text-based images and long-form written captions
+ image carousels displaying my architectural drawings and sketches
+ email newsletters with much deeper written content about particular topics or pieces of advice.

Whether through entertainment in my video production, education in explaining my workflow and portfolio construction, inspiration through my architectural work and advice or relatability with my monthly architecture photo dump, I focus on offering diverse content. This might include tips on managing time or encouraging students to care for their well-being – whatever the format, the goal is to provide value.

Figure 1.43–1.44 Examples of Thomas's content – 'Seven Steps to Pass Architecture School'.

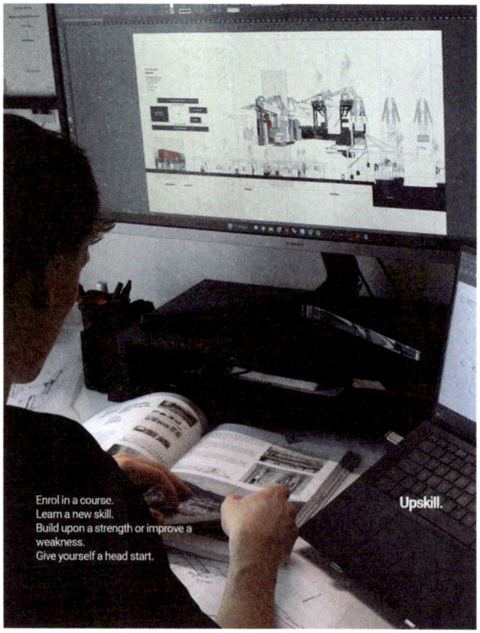

Content diversification allows me to cater to different audience segments with varying needs and preferences. Some prefer quick entertainment, while others seek in-depth tutorials or personal insights.

Moreover, this variety keeps the creative process dynamic and exciting. Constantly exploring new ways to communicate my message allows me to find fresh creative outlets and keeps the journey enjoyable.

PROCESS

Attention to detail is essential in my content production process, and I'm extremely passionate about the process of creating. I find my production value through the following components.

Figure 1.45 An example of Thomas's video content – desk set-up.

Figure 1.46 Behind-the-scenes of Thomas shooting content.

The Backdrop

My desk set-up – a monitor, laptop, keyboard, desk mat and various lighting – has become a consistent and recognisable feature of my content. I use greys, blacks and whites, with hints of blues and browns from my walnut monitor and laptop stand. Even details like the colour and material of my headphones, pen holder and pen are carefully chosen to create a professional and polished look. Whether filming in natural daylight or using artificial lighting at night, I've chosen warm tones that reflect my personal working preferences and give my content a calming, softer appearance.

Figure 1.47 Thomas's desk set-up.

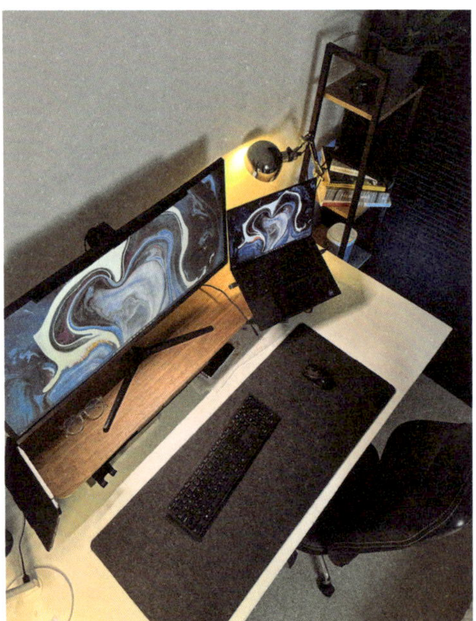

Figure 1.48 Thomas filming the 'Build your Graphic Style' course.

Shot Variation

Before filming, I usually sketch a storyboard to outline each shot, how I'll take it and the order of the clips. Even when I don't formally sketch it, I envision the shots. Shot variation is critical to keeping the content dynamic and visually appealing, as it helps communicate different emotions, perspectives and details. Here's a breakdown of the types of shots I use:

+ **Establishing shots:** These wide shots, often of me at my desk or in the studio, set the scene and give context. They're commonly used as opening shots to establish a point of view for the viewer.
+ **Close-ups:** I use close-ups to capture details like my face, sketching, typing or drawing. These shots reveal emotion and activity, adding depth to the storytelling.
+ **POV:** POV shots, particularly seen in my vlogs, simulate the viewer experiencing my day through my eyes. These are often shot at a wide angle (15mm zoom) to mimic human vision, giving viewers an immersive experience.
+ **Profile shots:** Side-on shots of me working add an emotional element and build anticipation. Often, the focus is on me while the actual work remains out of the frame. This builds curiosity before a close-up reveals the subject of my activity.

In post-production, I carefully edit these shots to match the message I want to convey. I edit to the audio, focusing on tempo, rhythm and seamless transitions to enhance the storytelling.

ACTIONABLE STEP

Efficiency plays a significant role in sustaining content creation over the long term. Each creator has identified a process they can sustain for a consistent stream of high-quality content, allowing them to publish content consistently and remain an active profile.

Methods for an efficient and sustainable content workflow are:

+ **Idea capturing**
  Having a location to dump ideas, hooks, titles and captions helps store and organise your past, current and future content. Suppose your content ideas often stem from the challenges, reflections or successes encountered while working in the studio, practice or daily. In that case, this approach will allow you to react and build content around real-world situations. If you don't capture ideas immediately, they're often forgotten. Use a free and easy-to-access tool like Notion to develop templates and document these ideas in real time.

+ **Batch production**
  If you are tight for time and resources, batch-produce content. Plan videos, prepare scripts, titles, hooks and storyboards before production, and then shoot multiple videos simultaneously. For instance, setting a camera on the tripod, arranging all the relevant lighting, and even doing small things such as formatting SD cards and charging cameras take time. By consolidating filming and editing tasks, it will enable you to manage content production in a busy life, including full-time jobs and family commitments. Save time by planning.

+ **Content repurposing**
  Repurposing content allows creators to reuse and edit existing content and reformat them to tell a similar message differently. For example, creators may often reuse a B-roll clip from a long-form video, re-purpose it for short-form content or capture a still for an Instagram carousel. The strategy is to build a library of clips, images or texts to draw from over time, helping to maintain a consistent content schedule without constantly creating new material.

UNIQUE SELLING PROPOSITION (USP)

While you can be authentic, create brilliant-looking content and craft a compelling message, it might not be enough if there's nothing inherently unique or eye-catching about your content. To demonstrate from the profiles we've seen, abby.architecture offers relatable documentation-style content but stands out due to her exceptional skill in producing architectural drawings and infusing humour into her content, making her unique.

Ross from Initiate Architecture speaks transparently about his journey to becoming a solo practitioner, establishing himself as a respected authority in this niche. Additionally, he films and edits his content to a high level of production quality, creating eye-catching and professional videos that make him unique.

Chris Simmons shares brilliant insight into the processes of being an architect in a positive and uplifting tone through conversational-style content. His distinct bright yellow colour palette and branding, which are eye-catching and easily recognisable, make him unique.

Each of these brands are successful because they have found something unique about their brand and content strategy that differentiates them from the rest. Considering why someone would watch your content over another's or follow you instead of your nearest competitor is crucial. A strong USP is designed to attract prospects even before they've decided to engage with your brand – it's about capturing attention and enticing engagement.

In *The 1-Page Marketing Plan,* Allan Dib presents a strategy to get new customers, make more money and stand out. While this book focuses more on building a marketing plan and improving product sales, Dib shares a compelling explanation of the USP. He states, 'You need to position what you do in such a way that even if your competitor was operating directly opposite you, customers would cross the road to do business with you instead of your competitor. Do it really well, and they may even stand in line overnight to do business with you instead of your competitor, like they do with Apple products.'[2]

You must immediately engage your audience, enticing them to pause, follow and interact with your content over others.

ACTIONABLE STEP

To define your USP, start with these five potential, unique attributes:

1. **Skillset**
   Do you possess an impressive skillset that is unique? Are you offering a skill you can teach or share that differentiates you from others? Identify what you do exceptionally well and highlight this in your content.

2. **Eye-catching work**
   Do you have a particular drawing or diagram technique, or are you brilliant at creating renders or visualisations? Are you an accomplished hand drawer? Are you an expert in a specific sector? Have you won competitions or awards for your work? Showcase these achievements and techniques to demonstrate your expertise and unique approach.

3. **Experience and knowledge**
   Do you have unique experiences or deep knowledge in a specific area? For example, are you an experienced architect with 20 years in delivering architectural projects, or are you extremely knowledgeable about generative AI? Leverage this experience and knowledge to provide valuable insights and establish authority in your field.

4. **Personality**
   Do you have a captivating personality trait? Are you funny, inspiring, a great public speaker or particularly empathetic? Let your personality shine through in your content to connect with your audience on a personal level.

5. **Unique service**
   Do you offer a service that no one else can match? Is there a compelling, unique product or service you provide that sets you apart from the rest? Highlight these unique offerings to show potential followers why they should choose you.

By considering these points and integrating your answers into your social media strategy, you can develop a powerful USP that helps you stand out in a crowded market.

ANA ARAGÃO

Ana Aragão graduated as an architect from the Faculty of Architecture of the University of Porto (FAUP, 2009). Currently, she dedicates herself exclusively to drawing, exploring themes of urban imaginaries and paper architecture. She has been part of many collective and individual exhibitions and projects, and is represented in collections worldwide.

SOCIAL PLATFORMS

+ INSTAGRAM
  @aanaaragao
+ FACEBOOK

MESSAGE

Ana Aragão's social media profile is fuelled by the creativity and individuality inherent in her art. Her atelier brand is seamlessly intertwined with her artworks, showcasing authenticity rather than strategic marketing. By sharing and documenting her work, Ana's brand remains genuinely unique. Her distinctive drawing style and impressive skill captivate viewers, making it difficult

Figure 1.49 Ana Aragão.

Figure 1.50 Ana takes inspiration from real and imagined architectures.

CONTENT TYPES

+ Image carousels
+ Short-form video (10–60 seconds)

not to appreciate her creations. Ana's exceptional expertise in hand drawing offers a powerful USP, setting her apart in the architecture and art world. The core message of Ana's brand lies in the authenticity and individuality of her works and drawing process. She explains, 'My brand identity has naturally evolved over the years, intrinsically tied to the artworks themselves. My social media presence has grown organically, serving as a window into my creative world rather than a vehicle for targeted audience engagement or promotional endeavours.'

Ana always conveys authenticity and artistic depth through social media stories, reflecting the most genuine aspects of her artistic practice. She explains, 'by focusing on the intrinsic inspirations and processes behind my work, I invite my audience to connect with the core values of my artistic journey. This approach resonates naturally with those who appreciate and find relevance in the authenticity of my art.'

Figure 1.51 Ana Aragão, *Já Eu*, mixed media on paper, 2024, 110 x 140 cm.

'Not a Real Architect, Not Purely an Illustrator'

Ana's position in architecture is unconventional. While the typical route in this field involves qualifying as an architect and practising within a firm, Ana has chosen a path that diverges significantly from this norm. She demonstrates that architecture can be explored through various means, effectively blurring the boundaries between architecture and other creative disciplines. This interdisciplinary approach allows her to create a unique blend of artistic expression and architectural principles, showcasing the versatility and expansive potential of architectural thinking.

By choosing a path less travelled, Ana has carved out a unique position within the architectural field. Her innovative and inspiring approach is a beacon for others who wish to explore their creativity beyond traditional confines. Ana's journey illustrates that finding creative license within architecture is possible,

Figure 1.52 The artworks display careful detailing in Ana's drawing process.

encouraging aspiring architects and artists to pursue their passions without being constrained by conventional career paths. Her success in blending architecture with other art forms and sharing it online has given her a USP that stands out.

She often describes herself as 'not a real architect, not purely an illustrator, which encapsulates the hybrid nature of my practice'. Ana believes this positioning 'allows me to stand out in a crowded space, offering a different perspective that blends the boundaries between different artistic disciplines'.

Distinctive Drawing Style

Ana's drawing style, which she calls 'paper architecture', and impressive drawing technique make her visually distinctive on platforms like Instagram. She states, 'If I could define something that highlights my brand, it would be the distinctive style of my drawings and the way I bridge the gap between traditional

Figure 1.53–1.54 Ana working large scale.

paper architecture and modern social media. My drawings are not supposed to be just visual representations but are imbued with a narrative that invites the audience into my world.' Her work stands out due to three key elements: scale, detail and three-dimensional quality.

1. Scale

Ana's drawings explore scale in two significant ways. First, she often works on large canvases/paper, creating expansive pieces that draw viewers into her intricate worlds. Second, she explores the architectural scale within these large works, presenting dense, overlapping clusters of forms that resemble bustling cities. This spatial complexity adds depth and invites viewers to examine each section closely. Such exploration of scale is captivating, and she documents her drawings well on her profile to draw the viewer into her creative pieces.

Figure 1.55 Ana Aragão, *Monopoly*, pen on paper, 2024, 29.7 × 42 cm.

Figure 1.56 Ana's cities hold intricate patterns.

2. Detail

The level of detail in Ana's drawings is extraordinary. While much of her work is produced on large-scale canvas/paper, she draws at a small scale too, infusing her pieces with vast detail and complexity. This meticulous attention to detail is emphasised by the large size of her canvases, making her work even more impressive and immersive. Each element is carefully drawn, creating a rich tapestry of architectural forms.

3. Three-dimensional quality

Ana's drawings possess a remarkable three-dimensional quality. She skilfully intertwines architectural references and spatial complexity using perspective and point of view to add depth. This creates a dynamic visual experience, making her work not only impressive in its technical execution but also captivating in its ability to convey spatial relationships and architectural depth.

Figure 1.57 Ana Aragão, *Tetris VI*, marker on paper, 2024, 100 x 140 cm.

PROCESS

Ana's content production process reinforces her brand's authenticity. She documents her work, often using her phone to photograph it, which adds to her genuine, hands-on approach. While this method supports her authentic tone, the artist emphasises the importance of high image quality to capture her drawings' intricate details and textures – see her high-quality photography. She carefully curates and edits these images to best represent the artwork, ensuring that the depth and quality of the original piece are maintained. This meticulous process highlights her dedication to authenticity and excellence in showcasing her art. She explains, 'I do not hire film crew or use elaborate set-ups, as I believe simplicity and authenticity are key to connecting with my audience. I believe that the success of this approach lies in its genuineness – each piece of content is a true representation of my artistic journey, shared with the intent to inspire and connect with others.'

Figure 1.58 Ana working on *Velasca Tower*, ballpoint pen on paper, 2023, 130 x 100 cm.

Figure 1.59 Books are crucial to Ana's creative process.

NICHING

In social media terms, a niche categorises your content and defines where it fits among the vast online content landscape. Some might see it as pigeonholing, but it's a highly valuable strategy, especially when exploring the right niche. Niching is a strategic approach to content creation, focusing on a tightly defined portion of a subcategory within a broader category.

Health and wellness is a niche. Women's fashion is a niche. Pet owners is a niche. These examples of niches are major – but still are smaller segments within larger markets, defined by specific needs, preferences and users. These broad niches have been selected to illustrate how vast they can be but with many subcategories within them. For instance, health and wellness is an expansive niche, making it challenging to establish a brand due to heavy competition. However, focusing on a subcategory, such as plant-based milk alternatives, presents a more manageable opportunity to solidify your place in that space. Likewise, within the pet owners' niche, focusing on subcategories like smart pet cameras or designer pet clothing allows you to be more specific with your messaging. By narrowing your focus, you can better define your target audience and communicate the unique solution or product you offer.

The idea is to narrow your focus and provide a specific solution to a specific audience, making it easier for people to find you and connect with your brand values. As Allan Dib describes it, you need to harness the power of focus.[3]

Architectural design is a niche. Architectural drawing is a niche. Sustainable architecture is a niche.

Once again, these niches are vast and already pretty competitive. Focus on narrowing down the niche you wish to explore. For instance, someone interested in architecture might look for content related to:

+ architectural fine line drawing
+ interior design and material pallets
+ visualisation software guides and how-to tutorials
+ generative AI visualisations and imagery.

By narrowing the focus to one of these areas, you can develop specialised expertise and become an authoritative figure in the niche. This approach allows for creating highly targeted content that meets a demanding audience's specific needs and interests, leaning towards high engagement and a stronger community. By being a big fish in a small pond, you can dominate the category, building a reputation as a go-to resource for that specific type of content.

TIM FU

Designer and founder of Studio Tim Fu, Tim Fu is a renowned designer known for using advanced computation and artificial intelligence (AI). Emerging from Zaha Hadid Architects (ZHA), he has since founded Studio Tim Fu, a high-tech architectural practice pioneering AI integration into visionary designs.

SOCIAL PLATFORMS

+ INSTAGRAM @ti.fu
+ TIKTOK @studio.tim.fu

CONTENT TYPES

+ Image carousels
+ Short-form video (7-20 seconds)

MESSAGE

Tim Fu, a designer and AI technologist, has built a significant audience through his innovative architectural work in artificial intelligence. Tim recalls that his journey into content creation began after achieving his career aspiration of working at ZHA, but as his ambitions began to drift, he saw social media as an opportunity to progress his career. He explains, 'I had seen some of our peers at ZHA obtaining exposure in social media, including Chantal Matar, Mariana Cabugueira, Filippo Nasseti, and a few others. Some were teaching digital courses, some were creating artistic content and some were being interviewed on YouTube. Their works were presented on various platforms and searchable online, and they have been invited to various talks and events. I realised the opportunity in social media to build upon my strengths and embark on a journey within content creation.'

STRATEGY

The 'Blue Ocean Strategy'

Tim has built his audience primarily by leveraging a 'blue ocean strategy', focusing on unexplored markets and content areas. Recognising that many creators in the architecture AI space were producing unrealistic forms and abstract interiors, Tim deliberately chose a different path to differentiate himself.

At the time of writing this book, the adoption of AI in architecture practice and education is still in its early stages. There's a strong interest in understanding how AI can be utilised – whether through image diffusion, text generation or other methods – to enhance various aspects of the architectural design process. However, many practices remain hesitant to implement AI tools or educate their teams on their benefits. This hesitation may stem from concerns about copyright issues, practices being stuck in their own ways or a general fear of how AI might impact the role of architects.

This is where someone like Tim comes in. He is actively exploring these questions and producing results that demonstrate the positive potential of AI in architecture, particularly in showing how AI can contribute to buildable designs and how it can be implemented effectively within practice. Tim hasn't just focused on creating practical, buildable architecture – he's also pushed the boundaries by incorporating a fluid, curvilinear design style. His time at ZHA has influenced his text-to-image generative AI work, as much of his content features this flowing, futuristic aesthetic.

Figure 1.60 Tim Fu.

Figure 1.61 Tim's AI creation on Instagram.

This combination of futuristic design with practical, buildable concepts allows Tim to create visually striking work grounded in reality. This fresh approach has allowed him to carve out a unique niche in a field increasingly crowded with AI-generated abstract architecture. While pursuing this 'blue ocean strategy' involves risks, such as venturing into uncharted territory, Tim experimented with numerous approaches before succeeding. He began by creating parametric design speed-run reels on TikTok, showcasing famous buildings in 30-second animations, before transitioning to the metaverse when it became a trend without gaining much traction. He explains, 'Everything changed in July 2022 when I discovered Midjourney, a text-to-image generator. I began experimenting with it and quickly saw the potential for generating interesting architectural content. Realising that many people were interested in AI's ability to mimic Zaha Hadid's style, I clarified in my bio that I was connected to Zaha

Figure 1.62–1.63 Tim's AI creations on Instagram.

Hadid and started showcasing content in that style. This helped me gain recognition as one of the first to explore the niche of "Zaha Hadid" and "AI architecture", and it resonated with a wider audience.' By being one of the first to explore this content, Tim solidified his position as a pioneering creator in the space, building authority and expertise.

Tim's strategy accomplishes two key objectives. First, he addresses the pressing questions surrounding AI in the architecture profession. By demonstrating real-world applications of AI, he is offering a much-needed solution to the demand within the profession for understanding and integrating AI into architectural practice.

Secondly, Tim is tapping into a highly relevant and trending topic. The rise of text-to-image architecture imagery has captured the imagination of professionals and the general

Figure 1.64 The London design team at Studio Tim Fu.

public, sparking a universal conversation about the potential of these AI tools. People have been amazed by the outcomes of these text-to-image software programs, which have generated widespread interest and curiosity.

This is where timing became crucial to Tim's strategy. If he had started a year earlier, his content might not have been as relevant or as much in demand, as the technology was still in its infancy. On the other hand, if he had waited another year, someone else might have already seized the opportunity to create realistic yet futuristic AI-generated architectural visuals. By launching his content at just the right moment, Tim was able to catch the wave of the AI trend and provide a solution that resonated with the growing interest in text-to-image technology.

Figure 1.65 Tim at a conference in Brussels.

PROCESS

Tim's process behind his content production revolves heavily around creating his AI-generated imagery. He offers valuable insights into his AI workflow, breaking it down into four key stages:

1. Concept ideation with Midjourney

The process starts with generating creative ideas using tools like Midjourney. These are called creative AIs. Tim inputs text descriptions to quickly produce visually captivating images that serve as a foundation for his designs. While these images aren't detailed architectural solutions, they are a fast and effective way to explore various creative possibilities. He says, 'These highly creative and fast tools come with features that make it easy to refine and adjust designs, guiding them toward the intended outcome.'

Figure 1.66 Tim's AI rendering showcase.

2. Design development in 3D

After the initial concepts are created, the next step is translating them into 3D models, grounding the designs in real architectural considerations like site conditions and building massing. Tim and his team develop these models based on the ideas generated in Midjourney, ensuring they are aligned with practical architectural constraints while retaining the original imagery's creative essence.

3. Re-rendering with AI (LookX, SUAPP Air, etc.)

Once the 3D models are in place, precision AI tools such as Stable Diffusion ControlNet, PromeAI, LookX or SUAPP Air come

Figure 1.67 Tim's research on AI as evolutionary algorithm in design.

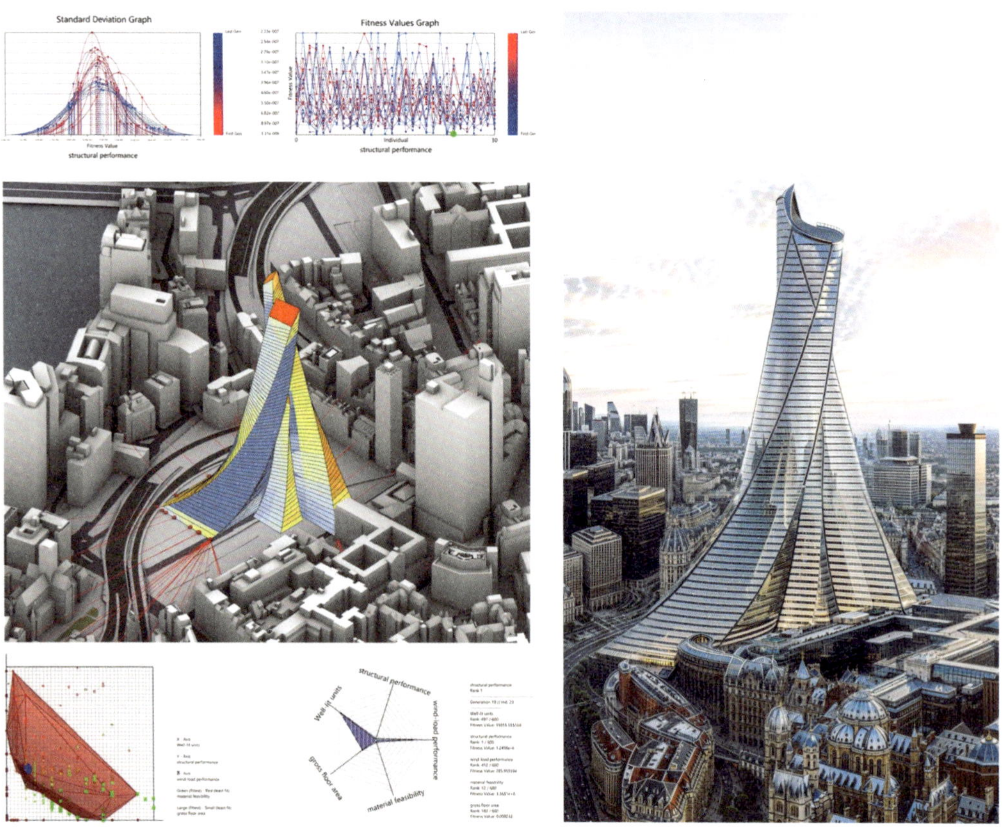

into play. Tim explains, 'This set of tools enables us to incorporate specific design elements, like a particular building massing, to guide the AI's creative process – letting it generate materials and details while staying aligned with the original massing.' Basic massing is transformed at this stage into more fully realised, visually detailed designs. AI suggests material finishes and other elements while staying true to the overall architectural vision.

4. Refinement with upscaling models

Finally, Tim uses upscaling AIs like Krea and Magnific to fine-tune the visuals, ensuring they're high quality and ready for presentation. Krea helps fix unrefined aspects, while Magnific provides enhanced realism and definition, creating a final polished and visually compelling product. Tim explains, 'These tools each have pros and cons that architects should consider. Krea tends to be more creative when enhancing images, refining rough shapes and introducing new detailed ideas, while Magnific focuses on providing greater realism and clarity.'

This current workflow is efficient, delivering high-quality designs quickly and precisely, but it will adapt and evolve as the tools do.

Personal branding has proven to be a highly effective approach to building a successful social media profile because it fosters authentic connections and trust with an audience. By humanising the individual behind the content, personal branding enables creators to stand out, be relatable and convey expertise in their field. This personal touch makes content more engaging, fosters loyalty and attracts professional opportunities. The flexibility of personal branding also allows you to evolve and grow with your audience, ensuring long-term success in a competitive digital landscape. Study how these profiles lean into their primary strategy while intertwining and layering multiple approaches. Each profile has its unique message reflecting its identity and brand, making it recognisable, memorable and approachable. Authenticity and consistency make personal branding a powerful tool for growth in social media.

A CONVERSATION WITH
MARIANA CABUGUEIRA [MC] STUDIOS

Mariana Cabugueira is the founder and CEO of [MC] Studios. She has carved a niche in the metaverse space, becoming a popular and authoritative figure for her explorative works.

Mariana explains that her journey in social media only became significant in 2018 and was driven by her desire for her name to be heard in the corporate nature of architecture practice while working at Zaha Hadid Architects. In my conversation with Mariana, I wanted to dive deeper into her journey of leaving practice and building her personal brand.

Thomas: *Mariana, what motivated you to pursue social media and build a personal brand? How would you define your brand message and identity?*

Mariana: I was a quiet creator until recently – 2018. The transition from quiet to loud came as an urgent need to resurface from the pile you are under in a corporate, creative environment. You can blame it on a lack of corporate acknowledgement, reward, space or the fact that you have never seen your name on your designs for three years. Instagram came as a medium to scream at or, in this case, create for. Twenty likes would not stop me from overnights creating for me under my name; it was my part-time job, punching bag or yoga stretch.

Since the beginning, one unique decision has been made here. I did not have a separate business account from a private account. My work was blended with my daily life, one as the backstage of the other, a natural, unfiltered reflection of my life, no tricks and pretentiousness, just me. In 2018, that was unusual for a professional, and controversial. It adds up to the fact that I am a woman, proud, and don't shy away from it.

Thomas: *What is your view on the role of content creators, and how do you differentiate that from the idea of the 'influencer'?*

Mariana: Let's be honest, *influencer* is cringe. It was cringe back in 2016 when we saw it surfacing, it is stratospherically cringe in 2024 while in its post-mainstream era. The *influencer* status was a title created by millennials and Gen X in the beginning of 2016; it is a combination made in heaven for a brand or person who needs to sell – our human need for capital – combined with the human innate trait which tracks back to early society, of *wanting* to be somebody – or *wannabe*. Influencers can sell while pretending to be, making you want to sell and want to be. This was my opinion when I saw the transitive verb being ruined in 2016, with my 100 Instagram followers and no Facebook account. This is my opinion, as I see the verb getting dragged in 2024, this time with 60,000 Instagram followers – and still no Facebook account. Nothing changes because we can all agree, *influencer* is cringe.

Thomas: *If you could advise someone on finding success in social media, how would you suggest balancing popularity with maintaining creative authenticity?*

Mariana: Influencers succeed in popularity and numbers; content creators succeed in respect and reputation. Both sides are valid; find your side – or let your art find it. AI has created an explosive long-term marriage between numbers and art for the first time in human history. As craftsmanship takes time and results in unique units, AI multiples quantity and shortens time, resulting in a diamond-shaped algorithm. Social media platforms, openly known for appreciating algorithmic quantity and/or capital investment, found skyrocketing growth through AI. So now you question your creative methods and your selling strategy. What is your art? How much can you feed an algorithm of quantity with it? This is an early decision: on the side of numbers and quantity or uniqueness and craftsmanship. The answer will always lie *in-between*, as slow-paced creations have less space in a competitor market and we have yet to see true uniqueness validation through AI.

If you are a creator and reading this book, I am guessing you want to succeed through your *art*. You want the step-by-step recipe to feed the insatiable algorithm of social media. But you forgot that the first and hardest step is through uniqueness. Unique methods, unique content, unique *you*.

02
GUIDE YOUR AUDIENCE

+ A Conversation With Oliver Uszkurat

Architecture is a profession rich in creativity, technical skill and problem-solving. However, access to education and professional development within the field remains challenging for many. Traditional architecture education, while providing a foundation, often falls short of equipping students and professionals with the practical knowledge, skills and industry insights needed to thrive. This leaves many keen for additional education and support, prompting them to turn to free and easy-to-access education. The rise of digital platforms and social media has created new learning opportunities, breaking down barriers to information and enabling individuals to develop their expertise beyond formal education programmes.

The evolving landscape of architecture education emphasises the role of content creators in bridging the gap between traditional academic structures and real-world professional practice – a role you can fulfil with your content strategy. It argues that digital education is no longer supplementary but essential in providing accessible, flexible and up-to-date knowledge for future and established professionals. Whether a student struggling with concept diagrams, a young professional seeking to upskill or an experienced architect refining their communication strategies, the need for accessible, practical education is more urgent than ever.

Through highlighting popular architecture-focused educational content guiding platforms like YouTube, Instagram, TikTok and podcasts, you will learn the different strategies to become a mentor, a guide and a positive influence on your audience, helping professionals navigate challenges, refine their skills and stay informed about industry trends.

This chapter is designed for you as an architecture professional, practice or individual interested in guided learning. It will teach you how to build a brand grounded on experience and knowledge, and emphasise your skill and expertise to build a deeper, more meaningful connection with your audience, making your content more impactful and memorable. The intention is to position the consumer as the hero – acknowledging their challenges and passing on your wisdom. By positioning yourself as a guide, you're not just sharing content but also offering a solution.

TEACHING VIA SOCIAL MEDIA

The first and most crucial step in building a profile focused on educating your audience is understanding and identifying your target audience. This means getting clear on their pain points (a recurring problem), desires and aspirations so that you can create content that speaks directly to their needs. This is effective with any educational approach, whether direct or indirect teaching.

For architecture practices, adopting an educational tone in content can be a powerful way to demonstrate expertise, establish authority and build trust with clients, collaborators and potential employees. By sharing insights into design processes, decision-making and project execution, a practice can position itself as knowledgeable, reliable and transparent – essential for clients seeking architects they can trust.

One practical approach is documenting projects through before, during and after videos. These could be structured as short educational segments that walk viewers through key design decisions, material selections and problem-solving approaches. Even at a high level, providing this type of insight helps potential clients understand the thought process behind each project and showcases the practice's attention to detail, creativity and professionalism. This type of content helps clients feel more informed and reassures them that they are choosing an engaged, forward-thinking and trustworthy architect.

Similarly, potential employees are more likely to be drawn to a firm that actively shares its expertise and culture. By offering insights into company values, project approaches and design philosophies, an architecture practice can attract talent that aligns with its vision and expertise – conversely helping the employee find a practice that suits them.

One effective way to define your target audience is by defining an avatar – a detailed representation of your ideal viewer. This could be a future client, a student, a young professional, a future employee or a collaborator. Defining who this is will allow you to tailor your message and speak to that person directly. Building an avatar is critical; we'll discuss this in more detail later in the chapter.

Here are some popular strategies to help you determine the best approach for your content creation journey.

STEP-BY-STEP

Step-by-step content is great for simplifying complex tasks into easy-to-follow parts. It is ideal for 'how-to' content, which seeks to break down the process of creating a drawing into each step, for example. A common strategy of step-by-step education is to show the before-and-after, an approach successfully used to show the creation of an architectural drawing or model, a construction sequence of a building or the building of a digital model. A step-by-step method could be sped up or slowed down depending on the pace of the teaching or insights.

TUTORIALS

Tutorials are similar to the step-by-step approach, and you can very much create tutorials in a breakdown style but, typically, tutorials will be more in-depth and comprehensive guidance on various topics. For example, tutorial content on using software such as Revit, SketchUp, and AutoCAD is typical and shows how to use specific features or complete everyday tasks.

CONVERSATION

Conversation-based content encourages learning through listening to conversations and direct engagement through Q&A sessions, interviews or discussions. It is a more informal and relaxed learning experience, where people can listen on the go or even engage in the conversation by asking questions live. Sometimes, this conversational approach doesn't require a conversation between two people; instead, an individual may aim to discuss particular topics informally and encourage conversation or reaction in the comment section from their audience.

LIVE OR PRE-RECORDED LONG-FORM TRAINING OR WEBINARS

Live or pre-recorded long-form training, such as courses or membership programs, offers structured, in-depth education, usually behind a paywall. An online course may look like 'The Ultimate Portfolio Guide', broken into modules and lessons. These courses can typically be between 1 hour to tens of hours. Live sessions build immediacy and connection, while pre-recorded content allows learners to progress at their own pace.

WRITTEN EDUCATION

The art of writing remains and can take on many forms on social media. On LinkedIn, you can share articles, documents or text-based posts to share advice targeted towards a more professional audience, while Instagram and TikTok captions provide bite-sized tips alongside visuals. Newsletters allow for regular, in-depth advice, and documents can offer comprehensive guides or resources.

These are the more significant examples of educational content you will see on social media today. Consider your brand objectives – are you aiming to provide quick, easily digestible video content in a short form, or do you prefer creating in-depth breakdowns, tutorials or step-by-step guides better suited for platforms like YouTube? You might even take a multi-platform approach, offering different types of content across various channels.

Some encourage more intentional learning than others. While I would encourage you to select a few of these strategies, you may even look to use all of them to provide a holistic and comprehensive learning platform.

A prime example of an architecture practice embracing education as a tool for engagement and trust-building is Studio RBA. Through its connection with ArchAdemia, Studio RBA demonstrates how architectural expertise can extend beyond client projects into comprehensive education. While the two brands remain distinct, they create a powerful synergy, leveraging shared knowledge, experience and professional insights. The expertise of Studio RBA's architects has helped shape ArchAdemia's educational platform, while ArchAdemia, in turn, has elevated Studio RBA's visibility, showcasing its capabilities to a broader audience. The following profile highlights how this dynamic relationship fosters education and architectural excellence.

ARCHADEMIA

For architects, students, interior designers and archviz (architectural visualisation) artists at every skill level, ArchAdemia is your one-stop destination to enhance your skills, industry knowledge, confidence and career trajectory.

SOCIAL PLATFORMS

+ INSTAGRAM @archademia
+ TIKTOK @archademia
+ YOUTUBE @archademia

CONTENT TYPES

+ Short-form video content (10–60 seconds)
+ Long-form video content (5 minutes – 1+ hours)
+ Image carousels
+ Podcast – video and audio (45+ minutes)

MESSAGE

ArchAdemia is a comprehensive learning resource that aims to empower, educate and uplift students and architects. The platform's core identity 'is rooted in the belief that architects should be respected for their comprehensive skills, intelligence, and artistry. We want to rejuvenate the architectural profession, helping to address the next generation's key challenges by emphasising quality, professionalism and well-being.' ArchAdemia's messaging strongly focuses on education, aiming to be a go-to resource for students, young professionals and architects. What sets it apart is the real-world practice experience that the educators bring to the platform. The creators of ArchAdemia also run Studio RBA, a successful architectural practice that has been in operation for seven years.

STRATEGY

Comprehensive Approach – One-Stop-Shop Platform

ArchAdemia differentiates itself through its comprehensive approach to architectural education, setting itself apart from profiles that often focus on more specific areas, such as architectural visualisation. This broader focus allows ArchAdemia to attract a wider audience interested in various aspects of architecture education and practice, from an architect's day-to-day working life to project management and fee structuring to design and software mastery. Its unique selling proposition (USP) lies in this all-encompassing educational scope, establishing it as a trusted professional resource. As one of the only platforms providing such broad education, it has become an authoritative figure in the social media space and one of the first to do so. The name 'ArchAdemia' was strategically chosen, combining 'architecture' and 'academia', thereby reinforcing its authoritative stance and educational focus (see ArchAdemia's Instagram profile grid).

Some of its YouTube video titles are:

+ 'What's the best render engine for BUSY architects in 2023? A must watch!'
+ 'Top 5 Books for Architectural Technical Detailing'
+ 'ULTIMATE Survival Guide for Studying Architecture & Beyond | EP 9'
+ 'How to become an Architect with the RIBA. An overview of the path to qualifying'.

Figure 2.1 A snapshot of ArchAdemia's Instagram page.

Figure 2.2 An ArchAdemia podcast recording.

Perspective Within Industry

In addition to its comprehensive approach, ArchAdemia sets itself apart through its perspective as practitioners and practice owners. In the social media space where numerous people provide educational content, students and young professionals often question the credibility of knowledge and experience, and seek trusted sources of relevant professional skills, expertise and knowledge. ArchAdemia explains that 'our students can be confident that what we teach is what we implement in real-world practice. Our practice Studio RBA is thriving after seven years in operation.'

ArchAdemia recognised the increasing demand for practical education provided by professionals with extensive experience in the profession and has addressed this challenge by offering an education grounded in practising architects' current knowledge and experience. This approach ensures that students and professionals receive relevant, real-world insights directly applicable to their careers.

Figure 2.3 ArchAdemia's D5 Render tutorial thumbnail.

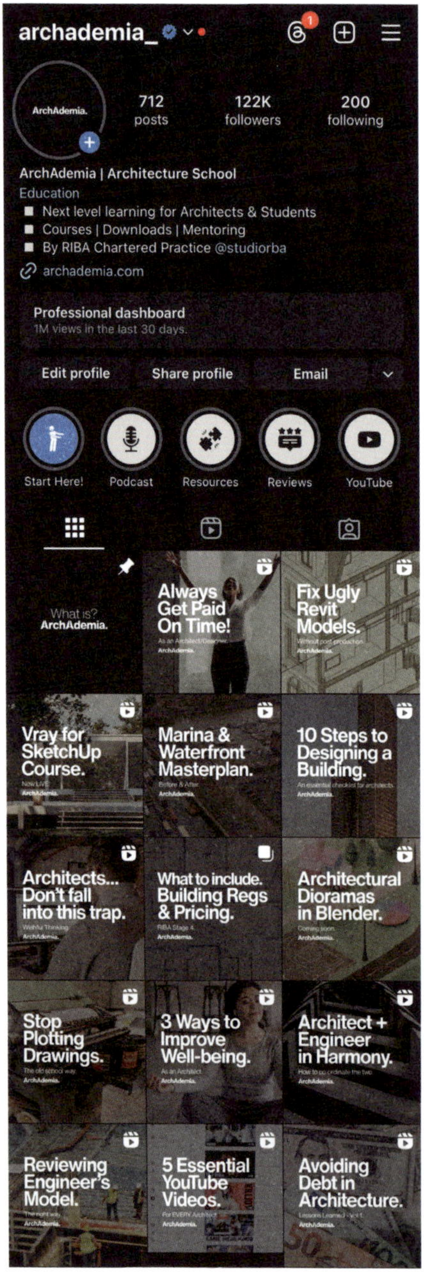

Figure 2.4 A screenshot of ArchAdemia's Instagram page.

Interactive and Accessible Learning

ArchAdemia uses multiple platforms to distribute its content to cater to different learning preferences and commitment levels. The strategy is to lean into each platform's strengths to maximise the content reach and engagement and make its content as accessible as possible. It states, 'Our premium tutorials are designed to be interactive, inviting submissions to our tutors for feedback and continuous learning. We alternate between long-form content, which allows for deep dives into complex topics, and short-form content for quick, focused lessons. This mix keeps our audience engaged and caters to different learning preferences.'

Instagram and TikTok

Short-form video and image carousel content on Instagram and TikTok is a feature of ArchAdemia's marketing strategy for offering quick and easily digestible education. Its content on these platforms ranges from design tips to myth-busters. It explains, 'A recent post combating the frustrating "click-baiting" around architects' poor pay in the industry has had 775K views! We've stated that in some smaller practices, architects' pay and working hours can be quite reasonable compared to other industries. The days of working for free and extremely long hours are becoming a thing of the past, especially with a new wave of forward-thinking, caring architecture firms and our practice is certainly one of them.'

Furthermore, much of this content provides insight and snippets into ArchAdemia's courses and long-form content hosted on its membership platform and YouTube channel. The strategy is to leverage Instagram and TikTok's fast-paced and visual nature to give potential members a taste of the value and depth available through its long-form YouTube and paid membership content.

YouTube

ArchAdemia uses YouTube for more in-depth breakdowns, step-by-step tutorials and podcasts. This allows for a deeper dive into complex topics and showcases the thoroughness and quality knowledge of ArchAdemia's content. It states, 'We've found that our content around visualisations seem to perform best.'

Membership Platform

On its membership platform, ArchAdemia offers additional educational content beyond what is available on its social media channels. This includes longer-form content such as courses, workshops and podcasts, which provide a deeper dive into various architectural topics. The platform operates behind

Figure 2.5 ArchAdemia's 'Architect's Portfolio' tutorial thumbnail.

a paywall, adding exclusivity to the available content and is designed to offer more comprehensive learning opportunities. The founders explain, 'This model fosters community and ongoing engagement, allowing members to continually develop their skills and knowledge. It also ensures that our content remains updated and relevant, providing ongoing value to our audience.'

PROCESS

High-Quality Production

ArchAdemia is known for its high production quality, particularly in its podcast studio, equipped with top-quality cameras, audio equipment, lighting and a well-designed studio set. To manage the production of such a diverse range of content across multiple platforms, ArchAdemia has streamlined its production process into a well-organised system that looks something like this:

Figure 2.6 A view of the Studio RBA office.

+ **Ideation:** Identifying relevant topics based on audience feedback and industry trends.
+ **Scripting/writing:** Developing detailed scripts to ensure clarity and instructional quality.
+ **Filming:** Recording high-quality videos with clear visuals and audio.
+ **Editing:** Enhancing videos with graphics, animations and supplementary materials to aid understanding – using Adobe Photoshop, InDesign and After Effects.
+ **Promotion:** Leveraging social media, email newsletters and their platform to reach their audience effectively.

Figure 2.7 Studio RBA team members curating a visual.

This is a typical production process for creators and is a good starting point for you to start your content journey.

In addition to its structured process, ArchAdemia recognises the value of spontaneity in content creation. 'Sometimes, our short-form content can also be instinctive,' it notes. Whether responding to a piece of relevant news, debunking myths, or sharing solutions to practical challenges, not everything they produce is polished and scripted. This blend of polished long-form content and more spontaneous short-form pieces has been instrumental in growing ArchAdemia's audience and increasing brand awareness.

Figure 2.8 Behind the scenes of ArchAdemia's podcast studio.

Figure 2.9 On air, during an ArchAdemia masterclass lesson.

DEFINE AN AVATAR

An avatar is a detailed account of your target customer or viewer profile, allowing you to tailor your content to specific demographics, interests, behaviours and demands. This approach is successful because it gains a deeper understanding of consumer needs and behaviours, allowing you to be specific with your solution.

This is an effective approach because it gives you:

+ **Precise targeting:** By knowing exactly who your audience is, you can create content that speaks directly to them, addressing their specific needs and interests.
+ **Better resource allocation:** Instead of spending marketing efforts thinly across a broad audience, resources can be focused on creating impactful content that resonates with a defined target audience, ensuring that marketing efforts yield positive returns.
+ **Improved brand loyalty and connection:** Understanding your audience's values and pain points allows for more authentic interactions. When consumers feel understood and valued, they are more likely to connect with your brand.
+ **Enhanced problem solving:** By recognising the specific challenges your target audience faces, you can position your brand as a solution provider, thereby increasing your standing as a trusted guide.

Creating an avatar requires you to think beyond the surface of your target audience and dive deeper into their psychology, preferences and pain points. The goal is to be hyper-specific.

ACTIONABLE STEP

THE PROCESS OF DEFINING AN AVATAR

The process typically includes:

1. **Demographic insight**
   Identifying key attributes such as age, gender, location, education level and income.

2. **Psychological profiling**
   Understanding interests, values, attitudes and lifestyle, including hobbies, passions and values.

3. **Behavioural insights**
   Outlining online behaviours, such as which platforms they use, how long they use them, why they use them, what types of content do they engage with and how they interact with brands.

4. **Identifying pain points and motivations**
   Understanding your audience's challenges and what motivates them to seek solutions. Finding specific pain points is critical in building your avatar.

To gather this information, analytic tools like Google Analytics, social media insights and customer surveys are used to identify demographics and behaviours – as you build your audience, your access to such data will increase. More importantly, a great source of information is yourself. From your experience during practice or education, identify your target audience's behaviours, pain points or motivations. Many of the education profiles in this book have built a profile around their avatar, reflecting on what they felt was missing with the profession and providing a solution.

Steven Rubio from Show it Better exemplifies this approach, crafting an avatar based on the skills, knowledge and expertise he sought but didn't gain from formal education. By becoming his own avatar, he directly understands his audience's frustrations, needs and aspirations. This deep personal connection has allowed Steven to create targeted, highly relevant content that resonates with others on the same path.

SHOW IT BETTER

Steven Rubio created Show it Better in 2016. He is an architect from Colombia with over 10 years' experience in architectural visualisation, design and content creation. He has been a guest lecturer at various universities and has worked as an architectural designer in numerous offices

SOCIAL PLATFORMS

+ YOUTUBE @ShowItBetter
+ INSTAGRAM @letsshowitbetter
+ TIKTOK @showitbetter

CONTENT TYPES

+ Image carousels
+ Short-form video (10–60 seconds)
+ Long-form video (5 minutes – 1+ hours)

MESSAGE

Steven, from Show it Better, has acutely identified his target audience and has built his brand with the primary goal of helping architects communicate their ideas more effectively – to show it better. He explains that during his journey through architecture school, 'I found traditional architectural education dense and cryptic, versus the education content I found at that time on YouTube. A channel called Visualising Architecture stood out to me because he [the tutor] explained many complicated things to do with representing our culture through creating architectural drawings.'

He adds, 'I was fascinated by this online education process because when you grab a ton of information and try to synthesise it, try to script it out, try to sketch out of it, try to edit it out, record yourself, then edit it, once, twice, three times, you end up with a very synthesised video that has the important information in it. In this process I envisioned how to use YouTube to learn how to show my projects better and how to do it in a shortened and engaging way.'

Steven started creating content because he felt architecture education fails to teach students how to communicate their ideas visually. By experiencing this demand himself, he became his avatar and an example of his target audience: someone feeling they were receiving inadequate architecture visualisation teaching and wishing to improve their ability to visually communicate their ideas through easily digestible content from someone with experience and the relevant skill. Stephen explains, 'My goal is not to create the best tutorials possible or tell people to learn five programs for architects. My main interest is how architects can better show their ideas.'

STRATEGY

Showing it Better

Steven's message and goal are simple: to show it better. This straightforward message is a clever branding strategy because it's clear and easy to understand. However, this simplicity also brings a challenge: Steven must prove that he can deliver his promise to the consumer who landed on his page. With a name like Show it Better, he has to meet a high standard to convince current and future followers that they'll learn to improve their visual presentations by following his content.

Figure 2.10 Steven Rubio, creator of Show it Better.

Figure 2.11 A render of a maquette detail.

To communicate the idea of showing it better, Steven's content highlights three standout features:

1. The quality of his architectural visualisation is central to his brand and content strategy. Stephen showcases his expertise in various visualisation mediums – renders, digital drawings, collages and animations – demonstrating skill that captures the viewer's attention. To illustrate his talent, he often presents before-and-after clips of his visualisations, showing them in their raw, sketchy state and then their finished, polished form. This transformation intrigues viewers and makes them interested in moving from the initial concept to the final product, which much of his longer-form content delves into.

Figure 2.12 A section of 'Working Terraces' project.

Figure 2.13 An exterior render of 'Working Terraces' project.

2. Stephen educates his audience effectively and captures his process with high-quality production value. He focuses on high-resolution film, audio, lighting, colour and editing. This high production quality reinforces his visual excellence and communication message, further establishing his credibility and market appeal.

3. Showing his face and his personality. As discussed in Chapter 1: Building a Personal Brand, including your face and image in your brand is a key strategy to help your audience connect and relate to the content and you as a person.

Figure 2.14 A collage illustration of FAUSP (Faculty of Architecture and Urbanism, University of São Paulo).

Steven explains, 'I differentiate myself from others by being very personal with my brand. I show my face, who I am, and where I'm from. I'm a Latin American artist with a unique colour, accent and interests, which helps define my audience. People relate to my content because of these aspects.' He believes people from various backgrounds can create engaging content based on their experiences and contexts. He emphasises the importance of letting his personality shine through his work and always aims to keep things personal. 'Even when I don't want to show my face,' Steven adds, 'I show my team or workspace. This approach makes my brand much more personal than if I were just a regular creator.'

Being Adaptable

Show it Better adopts a multi-platform approach, providing content that can be adapted across various platforms. Steven explains, 'Adaptability is key. Since starting in 2016, I've learned the importance of adapting my message to different formats and platforms. The best strategy is to stay flexible, whether it's a 20-minute YouTube video, a 10-second Instagram story

Figure 2.15 Steven giving a lecture.

Figure 2.16 Steven's desk set-up.

or a carousel post.' This approach is common for brands as it maximises the reach and engagement opportunities of the content and caters to consumers' diverse needs and time commitments. Steven effectively adapts between social platforms through his structured production process.

PROCESS

Steven explains that his structured production process meets the production standards, and adaptability is demonstrated in the show's better content. His production process consists of four steps:

1. Maintain a list of ideas, categorise them and choose the most relevant ones to develop. For tutorial-based videos, outline key points, script them and plan visuals for each segment. Structure the narrative for story-based videos with a clear beginning, peak and conclusion.

Figure 2.17 Thumbnail of 'How MVRDV is using AI to design their buildings' YouTube video.

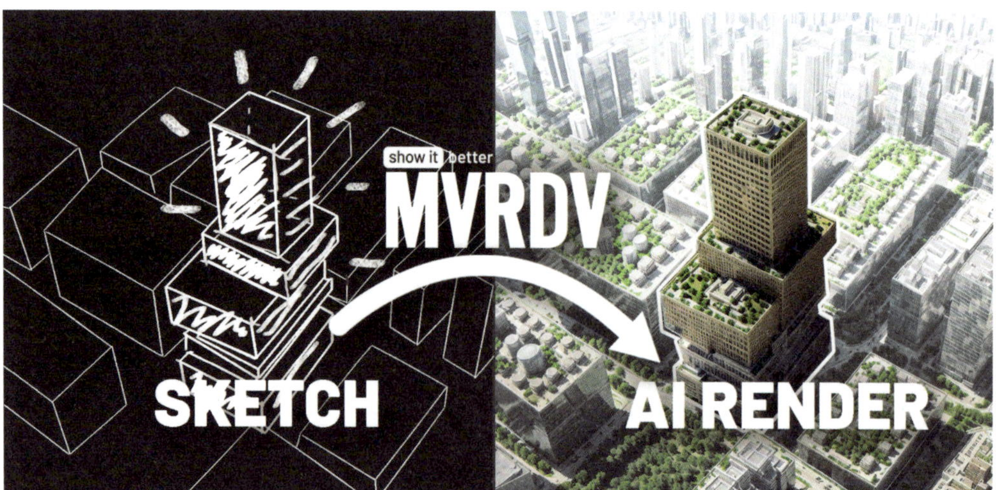

2. Record screen captures for tutorials, film yourself with a teleprompter for A-roll, and edit everything in Premiere, adding music, visuals and sound effects.
3. The editing process involves multiple revisions to ensure concise and engaging content.
4. Publish videos and promote through stories and emails tailored to their topic.

Depending on the video's complexity, Steven's process can take anything from a few days to a month. He explains, 'Initially, I used to create simpler, unedited screen recordings, but I've evolved to produce more polished, valuable content. The goal is to make educational videos that are informative but also entertaining and accessible.'

Figure 2.18 Thumbnail of 'Enscape Realistic Rendering – Full Workflow Explained' YouTube video.

Figure 2.19 Screenshot of a script for a YouTube video.

Script

I've been using Enscape since version 1.9, almost about...seven years ago, and Here are some videos and images I was making back then. Now...It might be hard to believe for the newer generations, but back then, this was really top-notch stuff... I swear!

Since that release, I've used Enscape for many of my projects and significantly improved my rendering skills! Today, I want to share some tips and tricks that helped elevate my renders from just okay to pretty awesome realistic renders.

Now, I don't consider myself the best Enscape user out there. In fact, if you check out the Enscape forum, you'll be amazed and shocked by the high quality of work some users produce. From interior to exterior renders, the possibilities with Enscape are endless!

But I like tracking my progress and feel it could inspire you, showing how you can better present your projects with Enscape.

When I visit the Enscape forum, it really pumps me up to try and match those awesome renders. So, if you're new to Enscape or wondering if it's for you, this video could really help.

Today, I'll break down how I created a series of images with Enscape, starting with a crucial but often overlooked step that applies not only to Enscape but to other software as well.

When creating an image, it's a common mistake to think everything needs to be built from scratch: new perspectives, magical lighting, figuring out colors, textures—the works! But that's far from necessary.

One key to success is starting with one or two reference images. These can set the direction for your render. In my case, I used an image from the 'Never Too Small' book, featuring 'The Warren'—a compact apartment in Australia with some really cool lighting, furniture, and overall composition that I loved.

I began by quickly drafting the space in SketchUp, modeling walls, floors, windows, etc. From my reference, I knew I wanted a portrait-oriented image of a living room with a yellow curtain in the foreground, vibrant large plants, a warm peach-toned sofa by a window that let in natural light, and a back wall with a wooden door, art frames, and other details, all over a tiled floor that caught soft shadows and a gold-covered closet to the right.

With this reference, I broke down my approach into four parts:

1. Create a detailed base 3D model.
2. Find quality 3D models similar to those in the reference image.
3. Texture the scene to match the picture.
4. Adjust the lighting and settings to mimic the original lighting setup.

Thanks to my reference, I quickly identified the elements I needed to start my image. And remember, don't limit your references to just architectural renderings. Photography books, movies, and interior design websites are great for finding inspiration.

COMPOSITION

Now, let's move on to our second tip.

Knowing our main composition, we need to optimize our 3D model accordingly. It's practical to avoid over-modeling and creating an excessively detailed model if we won't use all of it. This just wastes resources and time.

From the start, I save a scene with roughly the point of view and composition I want, so I can always refer back to it and track my progress.

I also set this up in Enscape, exporting renders from each stage. I just open my Enscape window, go to scene management, and adjust my scene, saving it also in my SketchUp scenes.

Understanding the main objects and their relationships is crucial. I like to sketch this out quickly on paper. This helps me grasp that the photo can be understood in three main planes, with a primary light source from the window and a focal point and balance at the door in the back.

MODELING

Before I share this third tip, let's look at some old renders I did and where I went wrong by skipping a simple step.

If you zoom in on these images, you'll notice many corners and edges look unrealistically sharp. In reality, most materials and edges aren't that sharp; they all have a sort of bevel to them.

Although Enscape doesn't currently offer a feature to round corners in the render engine, you can use plugins like RoundCorner by Fredo to soften visible angles in your models.

It's very easy: just select your edges, open the plugin, click on RoundCorner, adjust the settings, and voila! My window transitions from looking like this to this. Rounding the edges of this beam also enhances its appearance significantly.

Next, let's talk about sourcing your 3D models. Sure, Enscape offers a cool library of models and materials. Many of these you can tweak to personalize. But sometimes, you might want more customization for your materials or different models altogether. So, I asked my Instagram community where to find free, high-quality models for SketchUp.

While I got many responses, I particularly like two sites. First is CG Tips, a classic, straightforward, and completely free site. You just pick your model and download it. The second is Zeel Project, which works on a credit system, giving you a few free credits daily to download some high-quality models!

I also find that if you search well, you can discover great models in the SketchUp 3D Warehouse. But you'll likely need to create the textures yourself.

Figure 2.20 Screenshot of a YouTube video being edited.

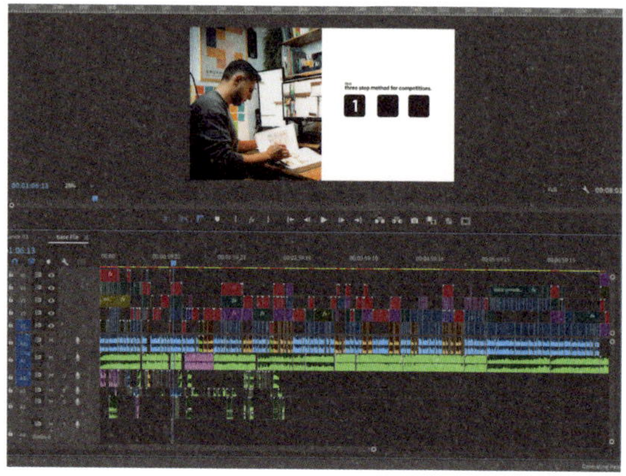

Figure 2.21 Screenshot of a weekly schedule of content creation.

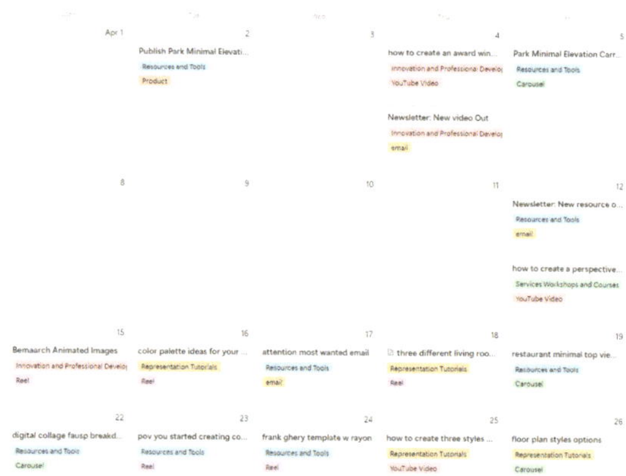

ARCHITECTURE CANDY

Vishakha Tiwari, founder of Architecture Candy, assists architects with visual communication, conceptual drawing techniques and curated design resources for creativity.

SOCIAL PLATFORMS

+ INSTAGRAM
  @architecture_candy
+ LINKEDIN
  Architecture Candy

CONTENT TYPES

+ Image carousels
+ Short-form video
  (30–60 seconds)

MESSAGE

The message behind Vishakha's brand, Architecture Candy, started as a simple idea: to be a source of drawing and visual inspiration for architecture students and young professionals. During her time in architecture education, Vishakha relied heavily on Pinterest for visual inspiration, such as drawings, diagrams and collages. Recognising that Instagram was becoming an increasingly popular platform for architectural references, she created her own space on the platform, offering a curated collection of visuals that could serve as a reference for other architecture students who were also searching for inspiration. Her profile is almost like a Pinterest board, a reference and resource of visual inspiration for students and young professionals. She explains, 'My goal was always to produce Pinterest-worthy images, which became a benchmark for me.'

However, the Architecture Candy social media content is more than just a collection of reference images; it is also closely tied to the courses and workshops she offers. The content previews what participants can expect to learn in her workshops. Vishakha clearly states, 'There is no ambiguity – what you see on the page is exactly what you'd learn in the workshop. Whether you're working on diagrams or concepts, you can look at my drawings for guidance. A wealth of reference material is always available to help you with visual communication.'

STRATEGY

Architecture 'Eye Candy'

There are two key strategies behind the Architecture Candy profile:

1. To provide 'eye candy' – visually engaging and captivating drawings. People admire these images and want to learn how to create them themselves. The page's primary purpose is to serve as a source of reference and inspiration, so Vishakha's drawings must be of high quality, catching the eye and sparking interest by consistently delivering visually stunning content, or 'eye candy', that meets a certain level of expectation. For Architecture Candy, the drawings and visual work must always be top-notch, ensuring they stand out and fulfil that promise of inspiration and reference.

Figure 2.22 Vishakha with her workstation in the background.

Figure 2.23 A sequence diagram.

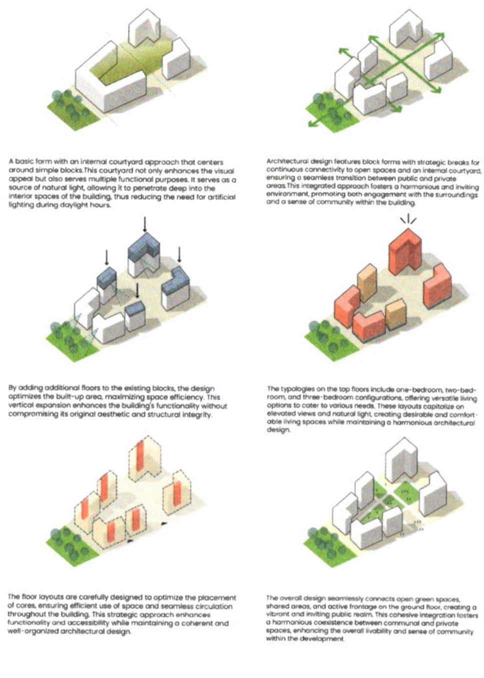

2. Over time, the Architecture Candy style has evolved into something easily recognisable – a minimalist drawing style combined with a vibrant colour palette. This was a deliberate choice to build brand recognition and offer a style unique to India and South Asia to broaden her reach globally. Vishakha explains, 'India and South Asia often have a very vibrant and colourful visual style, which can differ significantly from the more sophisticated visual communication seen in other parts of the world. I wanted my content to bridge this gap and offer a more globally appealing visual language.' The Architecture Candy brand has built an identity by adopting this specific drawing style and colour scheme, and consistently sharing content that adheres to it.

Figure 2.24 A site map illustration.

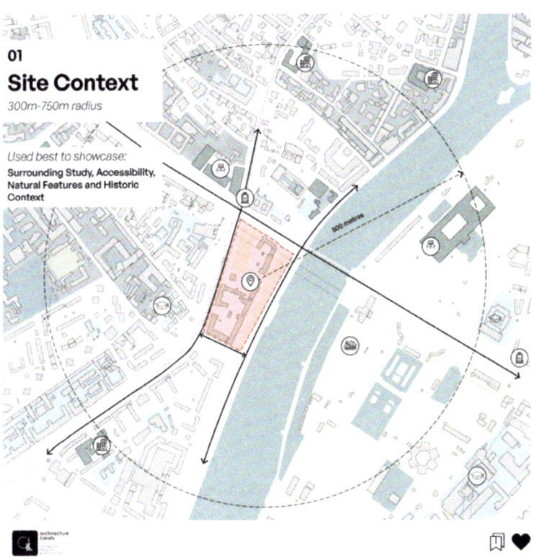

Figure 2.25 Carlisle city map.

Figure 2.26 An axonometric illustration in black and white.

Figure 2.27 An axonometric illustration in colour.

Figure 2.28–2.29 A self-paced course on diagrams on Adobe Illustrator.

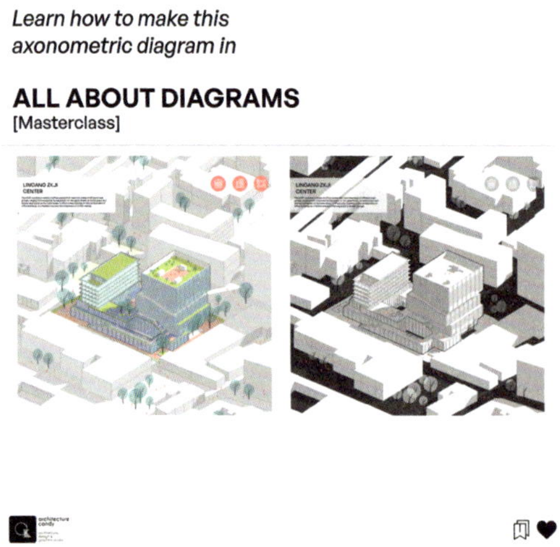

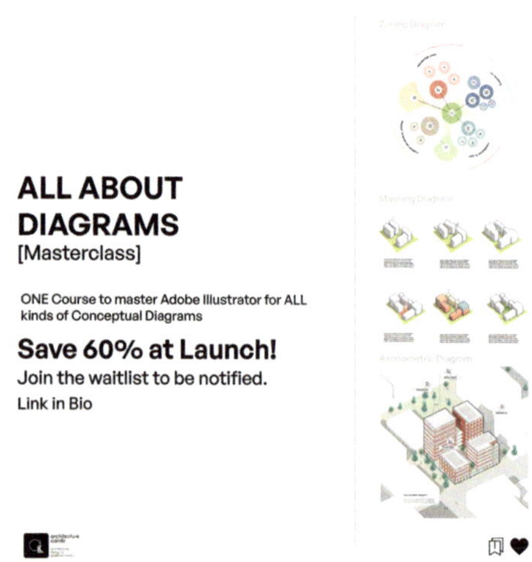

Workshop Focus

Another big part of the strategy behind the Architecture Candy profile is to build interest and encourage Vishakha's audience to enrol in her workshops. These workshops are designed to guide participants step-by-step through creating a drawing from scratch, with a strong focus on software workflows using Adobe Photoshop and Illustrator.

Vishakha uses various content types to keep her existing audience engaged and to attract new followers. Her goal is to inspire and provide a taste of what her workshops offer, ultimately encouraging people to take the next step and sign up. The main types of content she shares are post carousels and reels.

Carousels are particularly effective because they allow the audience to see different versions of the same drawing. For example, one post might show the drawing in the Architecture Candy colour palette, the next in black and white, another inverted

Figures 2.30–2.32 Process reel – text in 3D.

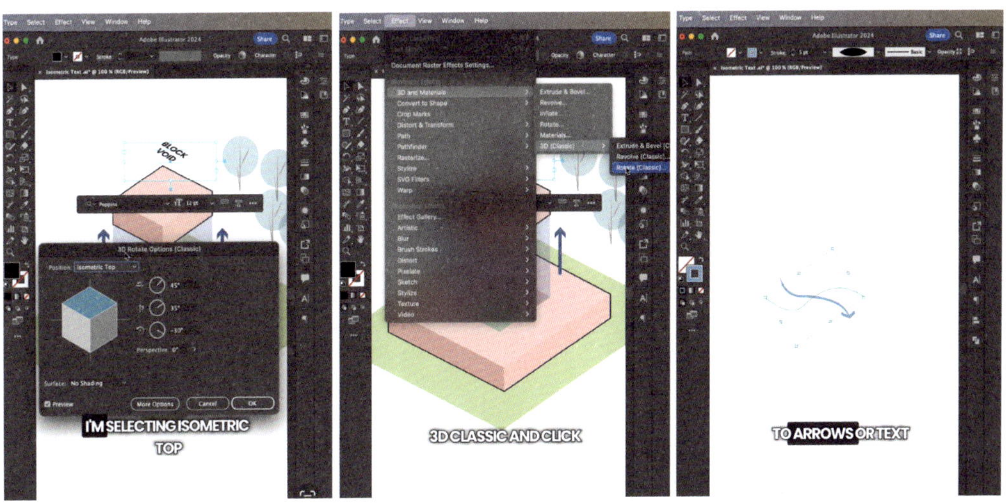

and a fourth with a different texture. This approach lets Vishakha showcase alternative styles and techniques, catering to the diverse preferences of her audience. It also highlights her versatility and ability to adapt to different styles, which appeals to a wider range of individuals interested in her tutoring and workshops.

On the other hand, Architecture Candy reels offer something different. Through short-form videos, Vishakha shows how a drawing can evolve when adding additional details or layers, such as shadows or textures. She often includes brief tutorials in these reels, giving viewers a glimpse into the techniques they would learn in her workshops – see Figures 2.30–2.32 for Architecture Candy reels.

These content strategies are designed to provide small, valuable doses of free content and education. The idea is to entice people with these snippets, making them curious and eager to learn more, ultimately leading them to enrol in her workshops.

Figure 2.33 A workshop in progress.

PROCESS

Vishakha explains that her content production process is straightforward and often spontaneous: 'I don't have a very elaborate process for producing content. I am impatient, so if I come up with an idea today, I usually work on it tomorrow and post it the next day. Sometimes, when I have many ideas but limited time, I jot them down for later.'

For instance, if Vishaka is browsing Pinterest and comes across an inspiring map, she might feel motivated to create one herself. She explains, 'It's a spontaneous and fluid process driven by what inspires me. For me, this is a creative outlet rather than a strict job. As someone in architecture, where creativity can sometimes feel constrained, this platform allows me to explore and express my creative side.'

Figure 2.34 Conceptual thinking.

Figure 2.35 Process and sketching.

CREATE CONVERSATION

A primary function of social media is to connect people through conversation. Conversations on social media happen in many ways, such as comments, direct messages, Q&A sessions and more. They can be constantly occurring between consumers and creators, or a mix of both. This facility of conversation is crucial for a profession like architecture. Conversations help break knowledge barriers, work as a team and remove the potential for gatekeeping within architecture. Online discourse allows people to ask questions to the right people, which wouldn't ordinarily be possible due to employment barriers or other obstacles. This open dialogue will enable individuals to be curious, discover more about the profession, and speak to people with varying levels of experience and knowledge in the industry.

ACTIONABLE STEP

1. **Ask your audience questions**
   whether directly or indirectly, asking questions is a great way to encourage discourse. You can do this through your posts, stories, comment sections or live features. When you ask your audience for their opinions or experiences, they feel valued and are more likely to engage with your content. Additionally, it can act as a feedback loop from your consumers.

2. **Talk about current topics or trends**
   covering current relevant issues is a great way to spark conversation. In architecture, for example, there is always new discussion regarding technologies, innovative design trends or practice/office culture. Responding to these will help foster conversation and keep your content current.

3. **Invite viewers to contribute**
   encourage your audience to contribute to your content through video inputs, questions for a live session or even user-generated content. When viewers feel like they are a part of your content creation process, they are more inclined to feel a connection with your brand. For example, designing challenges and competitions or questions or topic ideas for an upcoming podcast episode are ways to invite your viewers to participate.

THE SECOND STUDIO PODCAST

David Bruce Lee and Marina Bourderonnet are founders of The Second Studio podcast and the architecture and interior design office, FAME.

SOCIAL PLATFORMS

+ INSTAGRAM @secondstudiopod
+ YOUTUBE @secondstudiopod
+ APPLE PODCAST AND SPOTIFY The Second Studio Design and Architecture Show

CONTENT TYPES

+ Audio
+ Podcast – video and audio (45+ minutes)
+ Short-form video (30–60 seconds)

MESSAGE

The Second Studio podcast, hosted by David Bruce Lee and Marina Bourderonnet, creates a space for engaging conversations by having conversations. David and Marina are not just podcast hosts, they're also practising architects and partners in their architecture firm, FAME. The podcast started with a rebellious spirit, aiming to have raw, unfiltered discussions about everyday life, architecture and design. This transparent approach is still a big part of their message. However, since the podcast is intrinsic to their professional work at FAME, it also carries a more polished and professional tone. David and Marina

Figure 2.36 The Second Studio.

believe that architecture is frequently disguised in mystery, with most people not understanding what architects do. They explain, 'The architecture profession often operates behind a curtain, with most of the general public unaware of what we do, and many issues within the profession are not openly discussed. The podcast exists, in part, to bring transparency and to break down these barriers.'

STRATEGY

The Second Studio podcast is an audio and video show. The video content can be watched on YouTube, and shorter clips can be viewed on Instagram. The audio can be found on platforms like Spotify and Apple Music. Using video and audio formats is a common approach for podcasts because it allows the audience to see the hosts, the setting, and their expressions and body language. These visual elements help listeners and viewers feel more connected to the content. Offering both options lets people choose how they want to enjoy the podcast.

Figure 2.37 Screenshot from episode #407, '6 Reasons Why We Love Architecture'.

Figure 2.38 Screenshot from episode #387, 'Pros and Cons of Working For Small or Large Architecture Offices'.

Transparency

A core feature of the Second Studio podcast, which stands out, is its pursuit of transparency. David and Marina aim to educate their audience on various topics. Their commitment to open and honest conversations is a significant USP. They've identified a demand for transparency and open discourse in architecture, especially on important topics such as the role of an architect, work culture and relationships, and the design process. They explain, 'We cover a wide range of topics ranging from architecture critiques, design education, and advice for clients and fellow architects to discussions about the profession and casual stories about our lives. Our guests and listeners are equally diverse, including students, architects, interior designers, contractors and clients.' While this broader target audience approach can be more challenging for building an audience, it has proven fruitful, allowing them to speak on various topics without feeling tied to a particular architecture niche.

Figure 2.39 An episode cover for social media.

Free-Form Conversations

To create natural and unscripted conversations, David and Marina deliberately avoid sending questions to their guests beforehand, to encourage spontaneous and authentic dialogue. They explain, 'The more spontaneous we can be, the better. Some of our early interviews were almost three hours long because we wanted to reach a point where guests had exhausted their pre-rehearsed responses. Our interviews are still long, but after 400 episodes, we've learned how to push guests outside their comfort zones more quickly. This improvised approach might sound daunting, but honestly, we ask the questions that arise at the moment.' This approach has created genuine conversation, which people in architecture appreciate among the ambiguous and gatekept nature of architecture education and practice. It reflects The Second Studio's brand message of transparency and openness, cementing their intention of providing relatable, educational and enjoyable content.

Figure 2.40 Behind the scenes with Mike Riscica – The Young Architect.

Practice Perspective

David and Marina's active roles as practising architects and business owners give The Second Studio podcast many unique advantages. While a lot of architecture podcasts are out there, few are hosted by architects actively engaged in the field. This USP helps their podcast stand out as 'one of a kind'. Being current practitioners allows David and Marina to stay up-to-date with the latest trends and relevant topics in architecture. They can speak from personal experience, making their conversations more relatable and their advice more practical. Their active involvement in the profession ensures the content is relevant and deeply informed by real-world practice. Furthermore, running their own architecture practice, FAME, gives David and Marina a broad understanding of the day-to-day life of an architect and the business side of architecture. This dual perspective allows them to cover a wide range of topics within the industry. Their holistic approach means they can provide valuable content to individuals at different stages of their

Figure 2.41 Preparing for recording.

Figure 2.42 Behind the scenes with Dana Cuff, Professor at UCLA (University of California, Los Angeles.)

careers, from students and young professionals to seasoned architects and business owners.

PROCESS

With much on their plate as practice owners and podcast hosts, David and Marina have streamlined their workflow and hired an editor to help alleviate all the calendar coordination, booking, editing, publishing and social media tasks they used to do themselves. They state, 'This transition has been the most significant, allowing us more time to think about the show on a macro scale. Guests are booked two to three months in advance, and their episodes usually come out another two to three months after the recording. This approach ensures a consistent posting schedule but can feel odd since new releases seem old to us.'

Figure 2.43 An episode cover for YouTube.

Figure 2.44 Installing sound panels in the studio.

Figure 2.45 Fabricating base traps.

Figure 2.46 Marina, pensive during the studio installation.

Figure 2.47 Installing felt covers in the studio.

BLESSEDARCH

Creator and influencer Rishabh Wadhwa, an architect since 2018, touches the realms of design and architecture through his social media platforms collectively known as Blessedarch. With over 400,000 followers across platforms, he offers a futuristic perspective, guiding young designers with insights from global professionals.

SOCIAL PLATFORMS

+ INSTAGRAM @blessedarch
+ YOUTUBE @blessedarch
+ TIKTOK @blessedarch
+ LINKEDIN Blessedarch

CONTENT TYPES

+ Short-form video (30–60 seconds)
+ Long-form video (5 minutes – 1+ hours)
+ Image carousels

MESSAGE

Rishabh Wadhwa, the creator of the Blessedarch brand, tells stories about spaces and the people who design them. Initially, it started as just his personal brand, where his content focused on helping students and architects navigate architecture and design. He explains, 'Blessedarch grows with me as I grow. The core message remains the same, talking about architecture and reaching as many people as possible.'

Today, Blessedarch has become a platform that discusses architecture and design, with Rishabh still very much the face of the brand, capturing and telling stories about architecture as he visits different places around the world.

STRATEGY

Rishabh has two main strategies for creating content that connects with his audience and helps build a strong community around his brand: storytelling and community building.

'Tell Stories of Spaces and the People Who Design Them'

The first core strategy of Blessedarch is storytelling, which is at the heart of Rishabh's content strategy and style. Storytelling is crucial to how he talks about spaces and the people who design them. He believes that 'Storytelling is a good strategy in life, not just on social media. If you can craft a good story, you'll always be valued. Good stories and narratives connect with people better. For example, I wanted to connect with people when creating content about Norman Foster's home for refugees. Instead of just describing the house, I crafted the story to highlight the refugee crisis first. Effective storytelling taps into emotions, making the content more impactful.'

Rishabh tailors his content to fit each platform's unique style and algorithms, which means his storytelling approach varies depending on where the content is shared. For instance, his short-form videos on Instagram and TikTok are typically under 1 minute, requiring him to condense ideas and deliver them quickly to suit users' fast-paced nature and short attention spans on these platforms. In contrast, his YouTube videos, which can range from 10 minutes to an hour, allow for a slower, more detailed exploration of topics and more profound research into the subject, giving him the space to build a more elaborate narrative. Rishabh explains, 'All platforms are different, and different things are prioritised. It's like comparing weightlifting

Figure 2.48 Rishabh at the 'Amazing walk' designed by MAD Architects for the Milan Design Week.

Figure 2.49 Rishabh at the India Design ID Fair in Delhi.

to callisthenics – both exercises require different skills. I started with YouTube in 2014, making comedy videos, and later shifted to architectural content.'

To better understand the storytelling techniques Rishabh uses in his short-form content, let's break down his approach. Each video, regardless of its length, follows a well-structured narrative that combines audio, commentary and imagery to keep the viewer engaged from start to finish. Here's a closer look at the storytelling structure Rishabh employs in his short-form videos:

1. Hook (beginning) – opening shot and line

Rishabh starts each video with a hook. This is usually an opening line that grabs the viewer's attention with an establishing shot of Rishabh in the space he describes. For example, Rishabh used the line 'Did you know...' for some time in his videos, which became part of his content identity and something to make

Figure 2.50 Videos on the Blessedarch YouTube channel.

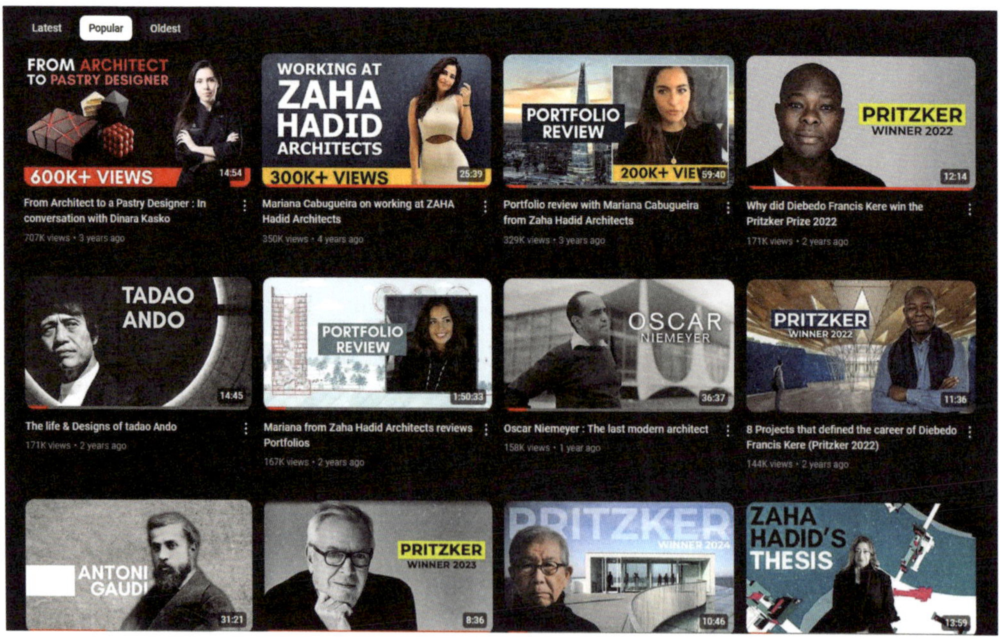

his content recognisable. Another example is, 'This Museum in Qatar is inspired by this rock' with an image of the museum overlaid and a cut to Rishabh showing the rock that inspired it.

The purpose of the hook in Rishabh's videos is twofold: it grabs the viewer's attention while also clearly explaining the video's concept within the first few seconds. This approach ensures that the viewer quickly knows what the video is about, allowing them to decide whether they want to keep watching – hopefully encouraging them to stick around.

2. Development (middle) – commentary and visuals

The middle section of his videos effectively develops the main idea through concise commentary and carefully selected visuals showcasing a mix of wide-angle shots of the space, close-ups of architectural details, graphic overlays and candid moments of Rishabh and other people within the space.

During this section, the commentary deepens, often explaining the design process, the inspiration behind the space or the challenges the architects face. The narration is well-paced, allowing viewers to absorb the information through commentary and visuals.

Figure 2.51–2.52 Conversation with architect Raj Rewal.

3. Climax/key insight – pivotal moment

Just before the end, the video often presents a key insight or a turning point in the story. This could be a significant design decision, a personal reflection from the designer or a revealing look at the project's outcome. For example, in a video where he discusses Antoni Gaudí's work and his journey of creating the Sagrada Família, Rishabh discusses the physical toll and impact the project had on Gaudí, leading to the ending of the story, which was Gaudí's shock death.

4. Resolution (ending)

Rishabh typically ends his videos by asking viewers what they think and encouraging them to leave a comment. This invitation engages the audience and sparks conversations in the comment section, allowing viewers to share their opinions and respond to the topics Rishabh discusses.

Figure 2.53 Videos on the Blessedarch Instagram feed.

Figure 2.54 A snapshot from an Instagram video at the Jawahar Kala Kendra designed by Charles Correa.

For Rishabh, storytelling isn't just a tool; it's a natural fit he uses to connect with people effectively. He points out, 'Storytelling is a natural fit, and I do it effectively. Good stories and narratives connect with people better.'

Community Building

Rishabh's storytelling is fundamentally a community-building approach. He intentionally crafts his content to help his audience connect emotionally with the content and his brand. This strategy goes beyond simply sharing information; it fosters a sense of belonging and engagement among his viewers. Rishabh actively seeks to interact with his audience by encouraging comments on his videos and utilising various social platforms to reach different groups.

He says, 'For community building, I communicate and connect with my audience through various methods like courses,

Figure 2.55 A snapshot from an Instagram video at the Alliance Française de Delhi.

Figure 2.56 Panna Meena Ka Kund in Jaipur.

interviews and portfolio reviews. This connection has helped me build a supportive community over the years.' By offering diverse ways for his audience to engage, Rishabh strengthens the bonds within his community and provides value across multiple channels.

PROCESS

Rishabh's production process significantly changes between YouTube and Instagram/TikTok. He explains, 'For Instagram, I keep things quick and dynamic. I start by scouting new projects and capturing photos and videos during my visits. The scripting is fast-paced, focusing on crafting strong opening hooks that grab attention. After that, I edit by layering visuals over my voice-over. If I'm focused, the entire process can be done in about 1.5 hours.'

YouTube, on the other hand, requires a much more in-depth approach. He explains, 'The ideation process takes longer

Figure 2.57 Rishabh at Panna Meena Ka Kund in Jaipur.

Figure 2.58 Recording a podcast at the UHA global office in London.

because the content needs to be well-researched and thoroughly planned. I break down the script into chapters, carefully crafting the narrative to ensure it flows smoothly. The editing process is also more intensive, involving multiple camera set-ups, voice-overs and meticulous work on elements like music, text and fonts. This process can take several days to complete, reflecting the more detailed and polished nature of YouTube content.' See Figures 2.58 and 2.59 for Rishabh's filming set-ups, either in his studio or on the move interviewing designers.

Positioning the viewer as the hero in content creation is an effective strategy because it addresses the audience's specific challenges and aspirations. By becoming a guide, content creators can help viewers feel seen and understood, offering solutions that empower them to overcome obstacles. This approach creates a stronger emotional connection, shifting the narrative from being about the creator's expertise to the audience's journey. When creators provide practical, valuable insights, they foster loyalty, trust and engagement, ensuring their content is memorable and impactful.

Figure 2.59 Behind the scenes shot of a YouTube video.

A CONVERSATION WITH
OLIVER USZKURAT UPSTAIRS

Oliver Uszkurat, the architect behind Upstairs – an international platform that explores the world of architectural representation and visualisation – discusses his USP and why YouTube is the core platform for guiding his viewers.

In my conversation with Oliver, I was keen to explore the origins of Upstairs and how it has carved out a unique space in online architectural education.

Thomas: *Oliver, how did you initially discover and continue to build the Upstairs brand through architecture tutorials and how-to content?*

Oliver: My journey with Upstairs (previously OU Graphics) began while I was in architecture school. I noticed how much my presentation skills (both communication and visual representation) made a massive difference in my standing out. Even if you had a brilliant design that addressed every need of the site and created something unique, it wouldn't matter if you couldn't tell its story properly. When it came time to present, if your drawings weren't strong enough to speak for themselves, all that hard work could go unnoticed.

As I realised the importance of representation as an architecture student, I also realised how little attention my university gave to this crucial aspect of our profession. I've always been creative and eager to learn software, so I taught myself how to communicate through images and drawings beyond the technical aspects. My classmates didn't have that same understanding, so I began offering post-class workshops to help other students improve their visual communication skills. This eventually led me to YouTube, where I could reach more students worldwide. I found that this wasn't just a gap in my school but a global issue; architecture students everywhere lacked these creative skills.

The gap between what architecture schools expect and what they teach, combined with visual communication's critical role in our field, pushed me to share more of what I knew. YouTube has become an ideal platform for delivering these in-depth tutorials to students worldwide. From the beginning, making a living out of it wasn't my goal. I genuinely shared what I knew and enjoyed creating videos around it, which is likely why Upstairs resonated with many people. It gave them access to valuable knowledge for free.

Thomas: *What makes your brand and content unique to others when creating tutorial and walkthrough content? Do you have a particular skillset, experience level or content approach that makes your audience gravitate to your content?*

Oliver: What sets Upstairs apart is that I've always focused on delivering concise, high-quality content. Instead of improvising or dragging out lessons, everything is scripted and refined before recording. I want students to learn these essential skills as efficiently as possible. This applies both to YouTube videos (so I can compete with entertaining content that often appears on YouTube recommended) and my courses, where students don't need to commit to a lengthy 30-hour course. Instead, they can take, for example, something curated like my 6-hour Isometric Diagram Masterclass and become proficient.

Being from Brazil also gives me a unique perspective on global economic disparities. Many creators may not understand how hard it is for people from regions with weaker currencies to afford international content. That's why I've always priced my courses and resource packs lower and offer discounts based on Purchasing Power Parity and for students. This ensures that anyone, no matter where they're from, can improve their visual communication skills.

Thomas: *With so many social platforms that offer various teaching methods, how and why did you choose YouTube as your primary social platform, and what strategies have you implemented to build an engaged audience? What features of the platform and/or algorithm have you utilised as part of your strategy?*

Oliver: YouTube is my primary platform for many reasons: Google's search functionality, ad revenue sharing, the ability to build a community, and more. It's a great place for creating long-lasting content. However, relying solely on algorithms or aiming for a viral video every time can be mentally draining, especially in my specific niche. So, I focus on creating content that genuinely helps students and architects worldwide while enjoying the process.

03
BRAND INFLUENCE AND COMMUNITY

+ A Conversation With Noris Obijiaku

Architecture is more than design; it fosters connections between spaces, people and ideas. The same principle applies to social media, where the primary goal is facilitating engagement and interaction. Yet, in a digital landscape with billions of active users, the greatest challenge for any creator or business is attracting followers and building connections and an engaged, active community. A true audience is not measured by numbers alone but by meaningful participation – people who feel connected, supported, entertained or inspired by your message. The goal is to garner an emotional connection between your audience and your brand.

Throughout this book, we've explored several key strategies that help you stand out and build a competitive edge on social media, including:

+ unique selling proposition (USP)
+ authenticity
+ niching
+ storytelling
+ defining an avatar
+ creating conversations.

These strategies are about giving someone a reason to follow you and engage with what you say and how you say it. From the moment they follow you and engage with the first piece of content they see from you, your community-building strategies kick in. Now you've grabbed their attention, the next stage is to nurture them, connect with them and share value with them.

This chapter explores the strategies behind fostering a community at any scale. More than just sharing content, it shines a light on building an ecosystem where your audience feels connected with your content, supported and motivated to participate. Through analysing community-driven profiles, we will highlight alternative methods to garner community engagement, whether direct or indirect. Furthermore, we will discuss the consequential rise of influence from social media profiles and macro-scale communities.

UNDERSTANDING ONLINE COMMUNITY

The difference between a following and a community must be made here. A following refers to the number of people who follow your social media page or subscribe to your channel, but it doesn't refer to active engagement with your content. Whilst gaining followers, exposure and views are fundamental to community growth, the distinction here lies in how a community implies a more profound connection where people interact with your brand and feel a meaningful bond with your message. A community is built upon shared values, motivation or goals, where individuals are connected through relationships and mutual interests. People are looking for people who share their values, who they can relate to and with whom they feel they can connect and grow.

In the online world, profiles that foster this level of connection and bond with their audience are the most powerful and promote fandom. This can be monitored through the level of engagement and interaction with your content through social media features such as likes, comments, broadcast channels, shares, threads, story replies and direct messages. These help facilitate and monitor discourse amongst your community members.

Focusing on community building offers numerous benefits for practices, groups and individuals. It strengthens your influence, amplifies your impact and extends the reach of your message – all while creating meaningful value for your audience.

Social media provides a powerful feedback loop that architecture practices can leverage. Its interactive tools enable real-time communication, making gathering insights, fostering engagement and building stronger connections with your audience more effortless than ever.

For architecture practices, this open dialogue offers multiple benefits. It provides an opportunity to conduct market research, understand the needs of potential end users and refine designs based on active input – acting as an extended public consultation. Involving your audience in the design process fosters a sense of co-creation, making people feel more connected to your work. Audience involvement could happen pre-, during and post-construction, offering numerous opportunities to engage with your audience.

Additionally, direct engagement helps collect real-life stories and testimonials, strengthening credibility. For example, sharing final marketing images or videos can spark discussions, with users sharing their positive and constructive experiences. This interaction not only enhances community engagement but also serves as a valuable research tool to inform future designs. Similarly, your audience plays a key role in shaping your content strategy. Those who connect with your brand can provide valuable feedback on the types of content they enjoy, helping you refine your approach. For example, they may prefer behind-the-scenes insights into your design process, model-making or workflow – content that gives them a deeper sense of access to your expertise. By receiving this feedback and data, you engage your audience and strengthen its connection to your brand, fostering a more engaged and invested community.

Community building is an asset to help build your brand and products, tailoring your message to the needs of your audience, forming a shared value and a motivation to follow and support your message. A community benefits the consumer and the creator/brand; there are conversing positives.

COMMUNITY SCALE

Social media's global reach and accessibility allow online communities to take on many forms and scales. There is a vast range of community types, some stronger and more impactful than others.

MICRO SCALE

You might have just a handful of close connections on LinkedIn – people with whom you regularly interact, who share your values and outlook. Even though this is a smaller, tight-knit community, it is highly engaging and you actively connect.

MODERATE SCALE

Your Instagram account might attract 20,000 followers with high content engagement who value your guidance, honesty and authenticity. Many of these followers actively participate in discussions, share their thoughts and respond to your content in the comment section, stories or messages, lending to a strong community.

MACRO SCALE

You might build a large following of 250,000 people across platforms, with a high percentage of them discussing with each other in your community group, subscribing to your newsletter, buying your products and attending live webinars and Q&As you host monthly.

For a social media community, engagement is king. You could have half a million followers, but the quality of your community could be poor if they aren't actively engaging with your content. On the other hand, a smaller group of 5,000 highly engaged followers could create a much stronger and more meaningful community.

In social media, there are many different types of communities. Here are a few examples:

1. **Networking community**
   These groups are focused on helping individuals build professional and personal connections online and in person. LinkedIn groups and connections are prime examples.

2. **Social media community**
   This type of community is built around a profile or individual through engaging, relatable and authentic content. Members of this community are emotionally invested in the profile and actively involved with the content.

3. **Learning community**
   These communities unite learners and students in one space, often centred around educational content. Examples include online courses, academic forums and study groups.

4. **Membership community**
   Operating on a membership model, these communities offer exclusive content, events or networks to paying members. An example is ArchAdemia, which provides access to specialised content and resources.

5. **Influencer community**
   These groups consist of like-minded influencers or role models who share advice and insights, and often collaborate on projects to support each other's growth.

Each of these communities has unique characteristics and serves different purposes and scales.

ALVIN ZHU

Alvin Zhu is a passionate content creator exploring alternative pathways in architecture, inspiring human-centric, functional and empowering design through digital platforms.

SOCIAL PLATFORMS

+ INSTAGRAM @alvinzhuxiyao
+ YOUTUBE @alvinzhuxiyao

CONTENT TYPES

+ Short-form video (10–60 seconds)
+ Long-form video (5–20 minutes)

MESSAGE

Alvin Zhu has built a brand around the core message of community empowerment. Through his experience and understanding of individuals' challenges and uncertainty throughout architecture education and practice, he openly discusses the complexities and ambiguities many students and young professionals face. With that understanding, Alvin's primary goal, as he puts it, is 'to support a global movement that prioritises well-being, fosters a sense of belonging and promotes collective growth for a better future in architecture'.

Figure 3.1 Alvin's master's thesis final project, 'Not Architecture School'.

For many, Alvin has become an advocate and a much-needed voice, championing the importance of community in a field that can be daunting and complex. To encourage this sense of community, he has crafted a personal brand that shares his experiences and journey through architecture education. He believes that as traditional career paths in architecture become increasingly uncertain, offering guidance and support to those navigating these waters is essential. Alvin uses his platform to share not only his experiences but also the stories of others. He aims to help students discover their unique paths in architecture. He explains, 'Documenting my path has humanised the architectural experience, making it more relatable and engaging, whilst authenticity also strengthens my connection with the audience.'

Figure 3.2 A still from a piece of content documenting Alvin's process.

Figure 3.3 Alvin speaking to an audience of students and graduates about the power of community.

STRATEGY

Vulnerability

Alvin explains that his strong sense of community and connection with his audience stems from his willingness to be open and honest in his content. We've discussed the power of authenticity and how platforms like The Second Studio Podcast creates engaging and insightful conversations through its unique transparency approach. Alvin takes a similar approach, believing that 'addressing both successes and challenges makes the journey of becoming an architect or designer more accessible and less daunting, especially for students and young professionals looking for guidance – something that the industry still lacks.'

Alvin's content showcases a level of vulnerability that has helped his audience build trust in him, encouraging others to connect and share their stories. A prime example of this transparency

Figure 3.4 One of the studio sessions recorded as part of documenting the process.

was his 'Co-Designing an Ideal Architecture School' series, which documented his final year project. Alvin discreetly set up a camera to film his tutorials with tutors and his critiques throughout the project's development. Sharing these high-pressure moments when his work was under intense scrutiny highlights Alvin's commitment to giving students an authentic look into what happens in architecture school. These critique sessions are often stressful and vulnerable moments where projects are on the line. This openness is unique to the profession and has made his followers connect with, relate to and appreciate his efforts to support the architecture community.

Actively Engaging with the Architecture Community

In addition to sharing his own experiences, Alvin actively encourages community interaction and engagement through various forms of content.

Figure 3.5 Setting up cameras to film a studio session.

Figure 3.6 Alvin's final thesis presentation to jury.

One way he does this is by sparking conversations in the comment sections of his posts. He often asks candid questions like, 'In one word, why do you want to leave architecture?' or 'Be honest, would you want your kids to pursue architecture?' These open-ended questions invite his audience to share their thoughts, respond to each other's comments and create dialogue.

Another way Alvin fosters community engagement is through video interviews with a diverse range of individuals, both within and outside the architecture profession. He explains that 'interviewing and engaging with diverse individuals has added a range of fresh perspectives to my content. I find great fulfilment in learning from others through honest conversations, and this approach has resonated with viewers who value genuine insight. By including voices from both within and outside the architecture

Figure 3.7 Alvin interviewing new friends during the Australian Design Review 30Under30 retreat in Bali.

Figure 3.8 Behind the scenes after an interview with Archimarathon (Kevin Hui).

field, I try to broadcast diverse ideas and solutions, promoting a more inclusive and informed community.' Interestingly, his interviews with people outside the profession resonate more deeply with his audience, often because the general public gives more candid and sometimes entertaining responses.

Storytelling – A Background in Film

Alvin's content storytelling and cinematic style are significant factors in the success of his community and brand building. His unique video style is deeply rooted in his background in film school and his passion for filmmaking. Alvin adopts a vlog-like approach, taking his audience along on his daily journey, whether moving from one place to another, setting up his desk or camera, or even going on holidays and trips. This approach creates a sense of intimacy, making viewers feel like they're a part of Alvin's day-to-day life.

Figure 3.9 Camera set-up on an 18-hour train ride during a trip to Vietnam.

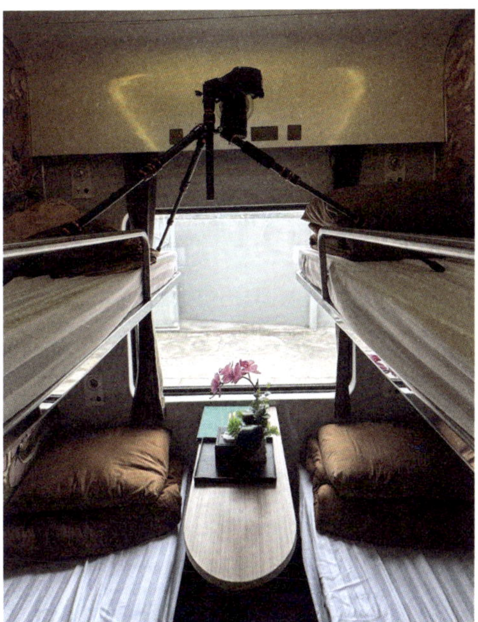

Figure 3.10 Interviewing new friends during the Australian Design Review 30Under30 retreat in Bali.

His love for film shines through in how he crafts his videos, using smooth transitions, point of view (POV) filming, and creative stop-motion edits. These elements give his content a high production value, yet he never loses the personal and relatable touch that resonates with his audience.

PROCESS

The production process of Alvin's content is a significant factor in the high quality of his work. Alvin's focus on production enhances his storytelling and allows him to communicate effectively through quality filming, audio and editing. Alvin explains, 'The process behind it all has arguably been my biggest strength in building the community. My content production process has been refined over years of trial and error, now focusing on two key factors: audience relevance and structure.'

Figure 3.11 Improvising when camera gear is not accessible.

Figure 3.12 Camera gear used to film studio sessions.

While storytelling is undeniably crucial to his success, Alvin emphasises that the story's structure can be just as important, depending on the content's nature. He understands that how a story is told – how it's framed, paced and delivered – can significantly impact its effectiveness, especially on social media, where attention spans are short. Therefore, scripting and structuring his videos and responding to market research are critical to his production process. He affirms, 'It has simply been a matter of asking people what they need and finding creative solutions or concepts and script that try to be both culturally relevant and structured for the social media age. The nuances of formulating content that aims to check all the boxes help keep me on my toes and up to date on everything social media related.'

Figure 3.13 Storyboard for a 'Critiquing Architecture School' episode.

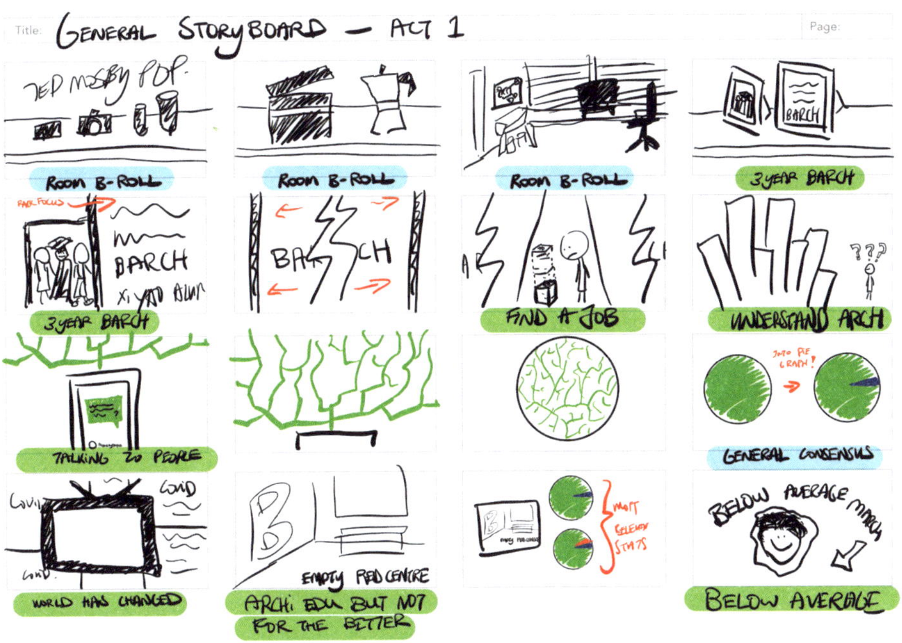

Figure 3.14 Shot list used during filming of a 'Critiquing Architecture School' episode.

POoR COLLECTIVE

Power Out of Restriction (POoR Collective) is a socially minded design practice that works with young people to create tangible outputs in their local environments.

SOCIAL PLATFORMS

+ INSTAGRAM
  @poor_collective
+ LINKEDIN
  POoR Collective

CONTENT TYPES

+ Image carousels

MESSAGE

Empowerment and Community

The POoR Collective is a socially minded design practice with a powerful mission: to empower young people by involving them in creating tangible changes in their local environments. Their core message revolves around believing that 'everyone has the power to make a difference in their community'. It focuses on amplifying the voices of young people, who are often overlooked, and works to ensure that their thoughts, feelings and opinions are heard. The collective states, 'We are trying to tell the story of the power of design and the importance of design skills, even if you don't see yourself as a designer.'

Figure 3.15 POoR's co-founders at Zetteler's media agency office in east London.

POoR operates with a clear vision and three main branches within its collective:

1. **Design**
   It collaborates with young people to create meaningful and impactful designs that benefit their local areas directly.
2. **Programmes**
   It runs initiatives to empower and upskill young people, providing them with the tools and knowledge they need to make a difference in their communities.
3. **Engagement**
   Through events, workshops, research and reports, POoR ensures that young people's voices are heard and acted upon, creating platforms for open dialogue and active participation.

Figure 3.16 POoR's *Architects' Journal* takeover issue.

Figure 3.17 Original graphic for Build The Way Traineeship founded by GPAD and POoR.

The POoR Collective's work highlights the power of design as a tool for change. Its holistic approach, combining design, education and engagement, creates a space where young people feel empowered to take action, use their creativity and make a lasting impact on their communities.

STRATEGY

The POoR Collective's social media strategy is built around three key components – Youth and energy, collaboration and physical engagement – each reflecting its vibrant and community-focused mission.

1. Youth and energy – bright and bold branding

First, the profile has been branded to match the fun and energetic spirit of the collective. Using bright and playful colours, it aims to create an engaging, lively feel for anyone visiting its social media or website, explaining, 'We want to energise anyone that visits our social profiles and website.' This energy and youthfulness are central to the collective's identity, as the four

Figure 3.18 A workshop image from POoR's 'Bexleyheath High Streets For All' project with We Made That.

co-founders – Shawn Adams, Larry Botchway, Matt Harvey and Ben Spry – are young, dynamic individuals. Their unconventional approach to architecture, focusing on empowering young people through design rather than traditional practice, sets them apart. They explain, 'While we are architects, we haven't simply set up an architecture practice – we started a design studio that champions young people.'

2. Collaboration

Secondly, collaboration is at the heart of POoR's mission to educate, mentor and empower young people. It actively engages with the community by co-designing, mentoring and using multiple platforms to extend its message. The collective believes in building spaces where young people feel they can shape their environments: 'We think it's important to build a community and platform for young people because often they feel as if they do

Figure 3.19 POoR's *Architects' Journal* takeover issue.

not have any spaces or cannot shape their environments.' These safe spaces allow young people to share resources, experiences and opportunities. The collective has worked with significant publications like *Architects' Journal, Dezeen*, RIBA, and the *Financial Times* to spread its message. These collaborations help boost its visibility and credibility, allowing it to reach new audiences, such as parents who can introduce their children to the collective.

3. Physical engagement

Finally, physical engagement is central to the collective's approach. Unlike many other profiles in this book that focus on building online communities, POoR emphasises in-person interaction with the community. Its social media profiles promote and share its physical work – advertising upcoming events, open calls and opportunities for students to get involved, explaining,

Figure 3.20 An event planning session with young people from Bexleyheath.

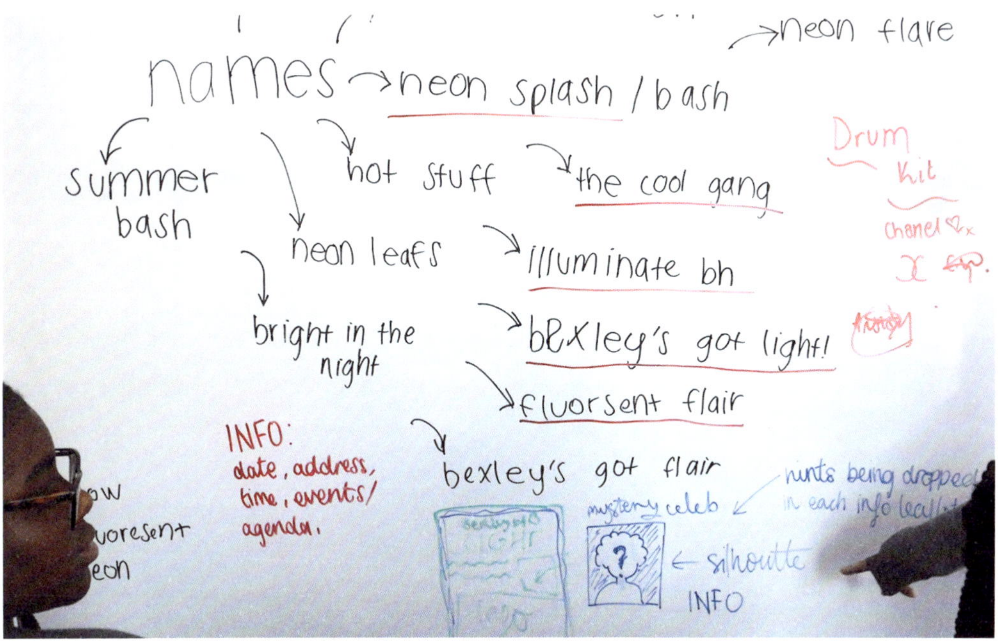

'We try to engage students by putting opportunities up on our social media platforms and making them aware of what is currently out there.' POoR regularly runs workshops, helps deliver murals and offers other hands-on design experiences to empower young people. Rather than relying solely on an online presence, it uses social media to amplify its real-world impact in its communities.

PROCESS

Documenting POoR's work is essential to the collective's profile because it allows it to communicate its community-focused message and clearly showcases its impactful work. This differs from creators who emphasise the production quality of their content; the POoR Collective places more importance on using high-quality photography and video that authentically documents its engagement with the community.

Figure 3.21 A mural design workshop with MA Architecture students from the Royal College of Art.

Much of its photography captures its direct interactions with the community, providing a genuine glimpse into the collaborative efforts. The collective also emphasises showing the behind-the-scenes process, sharing before, during and after images of its projects as it develops alongside the community: 'The process is always thinking about how we can help others. However, we try to lead by example. What we mean by this is by doing and showing how we did it instead of just giving tips or advice. For example, we will show you how we did a mural instead of giving you a list of how you could potentially do it.'

In addition to its project work, the POoR Collective is committed to platforming young creatives. It views its exhibitions as perfect opportunities to highlight new talent, ensuring emerging artists have a space to shine. It hosts opening events during these exhibitions that unite people from the community, fostering connections and networking opportunities.

Figure 3.22 MA Architecture students painting a mural in Mitcham.

GROWING INFLUENCE

As we have seen, community can be built by embracing vulnerability, engaging with your audience and sharing personal stories through compelling visual storytelling. On the other hand, community can be fostered physically by using social media to showcase your work and highlight the positive impact. Messages of empowerment and the opportunities they offer to engage with the community can be brought to life through social media platforms. Still, community impact happens in the physical spaces where you interact with people directly. Both types of community can be seen through the work of Alvin Zhu and the POoR Collective.

On a larger scale, audiences can grow to a much higher level with audiences of over a million followers while maintaining engagement and connection. As the audience and social reach scales, maintaining a community feel becomes challenging due to the sheer volume of interactions, making it harder to foster personal connections. If not careful, the intimacy and engagement that define a close-knit community can be diluted, and managing individual relationships or responding personally can become increasingly tricky. As you scale, it doesn't change the fundamental principles of fostering connection, belonging and support. In fact, as their communities have grown, these principles have only become more critical. The larger their audiences, the more global recognition they gain and the more influential these profiles become.

As your community grows, so does your ability to influence, leading to the emergence of the term 'influencer'. An influencer isn't just someone with a large following, but someone who holds the power to shape opinions, behaviours and even purchasing decisions. Their authority, credibility and connection with their audience give them the ability to inspire trust and guide their followers' choices, making their voice impactful across social platforms. Each profile in this book has a level of influence over their community – built upon their authenticity, expertise and relationship with their community.

The concept of influence becomes particularly relevant as your audience and community grow. As more people engage with your content, your level of influence naturally increases. With this expanded reach comes greater responsibility – your actions, words and choices are closely watched by your followers. Influential content creators like Dami Lee and 30X40 Design Workshop, featured on the following pages, who have gained global recognition, exemplify this dynamic. Their engaged and expansive communities give them significant influence, not only within their niches but also in the broader architecture community. As their influence grows, so does their responsibility to lead by example and positively impact those who follow them.

DAMI LEE

Dami Lee is a Youtuber, licensed architect and the owner of a multidisciplinary team, called Nollistudio, whose ultimate goal is to develop a general appreciation and understanding of our built environment, its impact on society and culture, and the hidden beauty beyond what the eyes can see.

SOCIAL PLATFORMS

+ INSTAGRAM @damileearch
+ YOUTUBE @damileearch

CONTENT TYPES

+ Short-form video (10–60 seconds)
+ Long-form video (10–30 minutes)

MESSAGE

Dami Lee is a licensed architect and YouTuber who has built an impressive global social media presence, amassing over 3 million followers across platforms like YouTube, Instagram, TikTok and LinkedIn. A clear and powerful vision drives her brand: to 'make architecture accessible to a broader audience and inspire them to see the world through a new perspective'.[1] This mission is at the core of everything she does, and it resonates with her diverse and growing audience. One element that sets Dami Lee apart from others in the field is her unique approach to content creation. She doesn't just talk about architecture,

Figure 3.23 A still from Dami's 'I visited the Autodesk Gallery and found this...' YouTube video.

she actively engages in the process of creating it. She brings the audience through the journey of her architecture project in California as a part of her 'project' series, involving them in the process of 'making' rather than focusing on the final product. She also takes advantage of architectural communication methods, like physical models, architectural diagrams and graphics across all her videos to discuss concepts.

STRATEGY

Universal Communication

Reaching a global audience means considering the diverse range of people you're speaking to and their ability to grasp complex topics. Many subjects Dami discusses are intricate and not easily understood by those within or outside the architecture profession. However, Dami excels at simplifying these concepts and making them accessible to everyone. She breaks down architectural projects to their essentials, ensuring that professionals and the general public can easily understand the ideas. Dami uses a variety of tools to achieve this clarity. Her

Figure 3.24 A still from Dami's 'I visited the Autodesk Gallery and found this...' YouTube video.

Figure 3.25 A still from Dami's 'Can this house slow down time?' YouTube video.

videos incorporate many images, renders, drawings, animations and CGIs. By overlaying and superimposing herself into the visuals using green screens and advanced editing techniques, she provides a comprehensive and engaging explanation of the concepts she's discussing.

Her breakdowns are comprehensive, covering various aspects of a project to provide a well-rounded, holistic view. Dami enhances her explanations by using references that connect complex architectural concepts to everyday experiences. This approach makes her explanations relatable and easy for viewers to visualise, allowing them to grasp the material more effectively.

Dami's YouTube videos typically follow a clear structure that makes them both informative and engaging:

1. **Start with a hook:** Dami begins each video with a captivating introduction that grabs the viewers' attention.

2. **Introduce the concept:** She presents the main idea or topic of the video.

Figure 3.26–3.27 Stills from Dami's 'Can this house slow down time?' YouTube video.

3. **Dissect the concept:** She takes viewers on a journey through visuals and storytelling. Dami discusses the project, concept or topic in detail, highlighting the pros and cons, challenges, implications and constraints. This often involves an emotional journey for the viewer, making the content relatable and engaging.

4. **Conclude, and engage the audience:** She wraps up the video by summarising the key points and asks the viewers for their opinion in the comment section, encouraging interaction.

This structured approach, combined with a rich mix of visuals, effects and CGI, makes Dami's videos insightful, captivating and entertaining. As a result, viewers are drawn to her content not just for the architectural discussions but also because they find her videos fascinating and compelling.

Figure 3.28 A still from Dami's 'SolarPunk Cities: Our Last Hope?' YouTube video.

Trending Topics and Popular Culture

In addition to her comprehensive video breakdowns, Dami understands that getting people to click on her videos in the first place is crucial. The title and thumbnail of a YouTube video are fundamental in capturing the attention of someone scrolling through their feed and making the video searchable.

A key feature of Dami's approach is that she creates videos around trending topics, relevant conversations and popular culture, which makes her content appealing to a global audience. By discussing topics like AI, manga, the metaverse, sci-fi and architecture in movies, she broadens the appeal of her videos, attracting viewers from various interests and backgrounds. This strategy enhances her video searchability.

For example, her most viewed video, titled 'This city concept breaks architecture (THE LINE)', has garnered over 5 million views. THE LINE is a unique and controversial project that sparked significant architectural debate. There are many discussions

Figure 3.29 A still from Dami's 'SolarPunk Cities: Our Last Hope?' YouTube video.

surrounding the feasibility of the scheme, its buildability, design principles, and environmental, cultural and ecological impact. This project raises critical questions about the future of architecture and the consequences of such a radical design.

Because THE LINE has captured global attention and curiosity, Dami is perfectly positioned to explore and analyse the project in depth. Her status as an architect gives her the authority and expertise needed to dissect the complexities of such a project. Her position as an architect allows her to offer a unique and informed opinion on THE LINE, making her analysis particularly valuable. This alignment between her expertise and the topic's relevance is crucial to the video's success. As a result, the video has sparked extensive discussion, with over 17,000 comments from viewers.

Dami's ability to simplify complex topics and present them through engaging storytelling has made her one of the biggest content creators, and one of the most followed.

Figure 3.30 A still from Dami's 'SolarPunk Cities: Our Last Hope?' YouTube video.

PRODUCTION VALUE

Beyond Dami's ability to capture millions with engaging, informative content and meticulous storytelling, her audience deeply values her high production quality and signature cinematography. Her distinct visual style sets her apart, making her content educational and memorable – a crucial factor in social media success.

Cinematography is a powerful storytelling tool, adding depth, intrigue and context to a message. High-production quality enhances the viewing experience, increasing entertainment value while reinforcing a creator's dedication to their audience. This level of craftsmanship is also a hallmark of Eric W. Reinholdt, founder of the 30X40 Design Workshop, whose globally recognised content exemplifies the impact of well-produced, visually compelling storytelling.

PROFILE SPOTLIGHT

30X40 DESIGN WORKSHOP – ERIC W. REINHOLDT

Eric W. Reinholdt's content is rich with educational value. He shares everything from his sketchbook ideas and model-making techniques to his iPad drawings, allowing viewers to see the evolution of his designs from concept to completion. But what truly sets his channel apart is the behind-the-scenes access he offers. Eric frequently creates content within his studio, discussing his workspace, desk set-up, equipment and the drawing tools he uses. This approach educates and inspires, as it demystifies the architectural process for his audience.

Some of his most popular videos include titles like:

+ 'Architectural Design Tutorial | My Process + Settings'
+ 'Updating My Workspace – Home Office + Desk Tour'
+ 'Sketch Like an Architect (Techniques + Tips from a Real Project)'
+ 'A Day in the Life of an Architect | Architecture Vlog'.

Figure 3.31 A still from Eric's 'iPad for Architects. Do you really need one?' YouTube video.

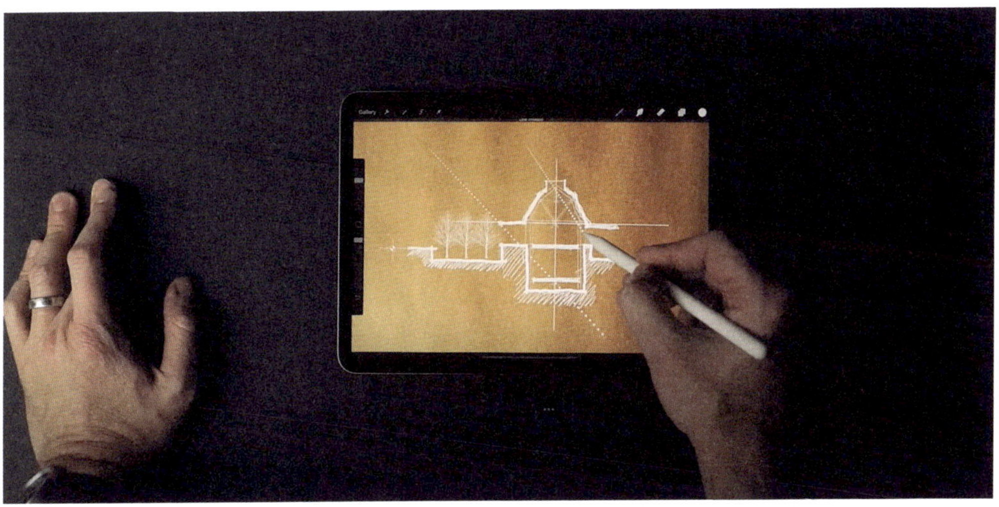

It's worth noting that Eric started his YouTube journey on 12 April 2013, with his first video titled 'Limestone Tile. An Architect's Take'. By arriving early on the platform, Eric was able to carve out a niche for himself at a time when competition was minimal. This early adoption allowed him to explore educational architecture content on YouTube, which is now prevalent in the architecture social media space.

Production quality is a vital feature of the 30X40 Design Workshop brand, placing importance on his videos' aesthetic quality and cinematic feel. His strong stylistic approach to content creation has led to a consistent production quality that has become a key part of his brand identity. From how he frames his shots to his use of lighting and colour, every detail is carefully considered to create a visually appealing and insightful experience for his viewers.

Eric's videos are known for their crisp, polished look, which he achieves by playing with focal lengths and depth of field. This gives his content a professional and cinematic appearance and adds variety to the visual

Figure 3.32 A still from Eric's '30 Minute Study Model – Here's How' YouTube video.

experience. For example, he often uses a wider-angle lens for shots where he's speaking directly to the camera, creating an inviting, conversational feel. When focusing on the finer details of his drawings, models or material samples, he switches to a more zoomed-in look, allowing viewers to appreciate the textures and materiality he's discussing.

For example, in his video titled '30 Minute Study Model – Here's How', several key production elements stand out, showcasing how Eric's attention to detail enhances his content and brand identity.

PRODUCTION DETAILS

+ **Multiple camera angles:** Eric uses multiple camera set-ups with different zoom levels to capture his models from various perspectives. This highlights the material feel of the models and helps the viewer follow the processes he's describing. The angles provide a comprehensive view, making the content informative and visually engaging.

Figure 3.33 A still from Eric's '30 Minute Study Model – Here's How' YouTube video.

- **Top-down shots:** A signature shot in Eric's content is the top-down camera angle, particularly when discussing model-making, drawing processes or material samples. This angle mimics Eric's point of view, effectively placing the viewer in his shoes and providing a clear perspective on his work. It's a practical choice that enhances the viewer's understanding of the content.

POST-PRODUCTION ELEMENTS

- **Voice-over commentary:** Eric's commentary on his model-making process is delivered via voice-over in this video, as in many others. This allows him to provide detailed explanations without distracting from the visual content. It's a technique that adds a layer of professionalism to his videos while keeping the focus on the process.
- **Smooth transitions:** Instead of using hard cuts, Eric opts for fades between shots, giving the transitions a smoother, more polished feel.

Figure 3.34 A still from Eric's 'Most of my time as an architect is spent doing this...' YouTube video.

Figure 3.35 A still from Eric's 'Updating My Workspace – Home Office + Desk Tour' YouTube video.

This subtle choice adds to the overall cinematic quality of his videos and helps maintain the viewer's immersion.

+ **Colour grading:** Eric's videos are also distinct for their consistent colour palette, dominated by blacks, greys, whites, blues and warm tones like oranges and browns. He uses a cooler colour temperature, enhancing the mood of his videos and reinforcing his brand's visual identity.

Eric has built a large, loyal audience over the years, earning respect within the architecture community through his consistency and transparency. His ability to maintain this community stems from his commitment to sharing valuable, educational content that deepens his projects. Eric's consistent production quality and attention to detail strengthen his brand identity. By providing real value and maintaining a high standard, he has successfully sustained a dedicated following that continues to appreciate and respect his work.

Figure 3.36 A still from Eric's 'Updating My Workspace – Home Office + Desk Tour' YouTube video.

Building a successful online presence in the architecture community hinges on more than just creating content; it's about fostering genuine connections and building a community around shared interests and values. The examples of Alvin Zhu, The POoR Collective, Dami Lee and 30X40 Design Workshop illustrate the power of authenticity, storytelling and a deep commitment to quality in cultivating engaged, loyal audiences. Whether through the intimate storytelling of Alvin Zhu, the real-world impact of The POoR Collective, the accessible yet insightful content of Dami Lee, or the polished educational approach of 30X40 Design Workshop, each creator has found a way to connect deeply with their audience.

Whether your goal is to expand your network, build industry relationships, grow a global audience or seek collaboration opportunities, the key is to ensure that your message is clear and authentic. Start by defining what you want to achieve and who you want to reach. Then, craft a message that aligns with your values and resonates with your target audience. Ensure your content consistently reflects this message; authenticity is crucial for building trust and connection. Engage actively with your audience by encouraging interaction and responding thoughtfully. Remember, people are likelier to connect with and support someone genuine and transparent. By staying true to your mission and consistently delivering value, you'll create a community that feels connected and eager to engage, collaborate and grow with you.

A CONVERSATION WITH
NORIS OBIJIAKU THE DESIGN SUITE

Noris Obijiaku, also known as Mr Chuck or The Design Suite, is an architectural designer, passionate about community design, exploring the ability to design spaces that positively impact people physically and emotionally.

In my conversation with Noris, I was eager to explore how he uses social media to highlight the deep connection between architecture, culture and community. His content is unique – educational, insightful and immersive – as he actively visits buildings, neighbourhoods and public spaces to uncover their impact on communities.

Thomas: *Your work highlights how architecture can build or weaken communities, primarily through neighbourhood and social housing design. Your content stands out as educational, authentic and unique. It often features on-site visits, like your 'Blocks in ends' series in London. What inspired your focus on London neighbourhoods and social housing, and why did you choose this direction for your content?*

Noris: It comes from growing up in council housing. Not in London – I moved here later – but my childhood town had a strong community vibe, unlike the estates I encountered in London. Those estates often carried a stigma, something I noticed even as a child. Bars on doors and hostile designs made the environment feel unwelcoming. I became fascinated with architecture's role in shaping these feelings, leading to my dissertation on the stigma surrounding council estates in London. Is it the people or the design that creates this perception? That question stuck with me.

When I started social media, I wanted to do something different, so I reviewed blocks and neighbourhoods. I wanted to challenge the cynicism around these spaces and appreciate their design philosophies. It's taught me to value the experimentation of the 1960s and 1970s, even if it sometimes failed. Those ideas – creating flow and designing for people – are still relevant. My content invites others to rethink architecture, and it's been rewarding to hear people say they now notice buildings differently.

Thomas: *Do you feel that your journey through social media has helped you find answers to the questions you explored in your dissertation? Architecture plays a significant role in shaping how people use and feel within spaces. Through showcasing and discussing architecture – examining why specific community spaces are designed the way they are – do you think you've gained a deeper understanding of these communities? And how does this journey help educate your audience about architecture and communities?*

Noris: It's ongoing. I've realised that architecture is influenced by politics, economics and policy as much as design. But I've learned that architects need empathy; we design for others. My content bridges this gap, sparking curiosity in people outside the profession. I aim to put architecture at the forefront of people's minds because many don't realise how much it influences how they use and feel in a space. Through my content, I've even had non-architects tell me they now question design choices, and this is what draws me to architecture – it's incredible to think that through design, you can create a space that genuinely impacts how someone feels. That thought alone puts a smile on my face.

However, the dissertation question has evolved. It's no longer just about whether it's the design or the people; it's about how we empower architects to prioritise human-centric designs over developer demands. That's the more significant challenge now.

Thomas: *Let's shift to your content strategy. You document your journey as an architecture student, share sketches and post diverse content. Why this mix, and how has it helped grow your community?*

Noris: My content reflects my personal journey. It's more about exploring my passion for architecture and inviting everyone to join me along the way. My approach has always been to focus on creating content that resonates and works – content I've tested and know engages my audience.

For instance, my sketching videos consistently perform well, and my 'Blocks in ends' series targets a different audience but is equally effective. That said, filming for 'Block in ends' is something I can only do every couple of weeks due to the time and effort involved. To strike a balance, I mix in more manageable content, like sketching videos I can create at home. This way, I maintain consistency while offering variety to my audience.

Over time, I have expanded into different formats – block videos, green screens, sketches – to keep things fresh. The variety lets me stay consistent without burning out. I aim to balance higher-effort videos, like my neighbourhood reviews, with quicker content, like sketching videos. It's about sustainability while still engaging my audience.

04
MONETISATION AND ENTREPRENEURSHIP

+ A Conversation With David Drazil

Now that you've built your audience and fostered active engagement, the next step is monetising. Creating content takes time, effort and resources, so it's only natural to expect a return. While some find satisfaction in sharing knowledge or gaining recognition, for many financial reward is a principal motivation; make no mistake, compensation for your work is an essential part of the equation. More evidently, for a profession such as architecture, which is known for its intensity and challenging cultures with arguably sub-par financial rewards, social media is both a creative outlet and a financial one for many architecture content creators.

The challenge? As a creator or business, the struggle is knowing where to start. You might have an engaged audience, but converting followers into paying customers isn't straightforward. The key isn't just having an audience; it's understanding how to channel value into an irresistible offer.

Whether you started your profile to sell a product or service from day one or focused on growing an audience first, financial success on social media requires a clear strategy. This chapter will guide you through proven techniques to monetise your platform, whether as an individual creator, group or architecture practice. You'll learn different monetisation methods, how to choose the right one for your brand and how to turn your online presence into a profitable business.

ARCHITECTING MONETISATION

As Austin Kleon candidly puts it in his discussion about artists 'selling out', 'Whether an artist makes money off his work or not, money has to come from somewhere, be it a day job, a wealthy spouse, a trust fund, an arts grant, or a patron.'[1] Architecture is a highly competitive field, with practices constantly competing for projects, clients and fair fees. The demanding nature of the profession often leads to overworked employees with financial rewards that don't always reflect the years of study and dedication required to become and work as an architect. Many professionals have little control over their work, limited ownership and frustrating financial constraints.

Social media and entrepreneurial avenues present an attractive opportunity for individuals to gain financial independence. Whether through content creation, digital products or brand collaborations, professionals can diversify their income and create new revenue streams beyond traditional practice.

Your audience must first find value in your content, and converting them into paying customers requires skill. Social media experts like Kleon, Alex Hormozi, Allan Dib, and Gary Vee (Gary Vaynerchuk) emphasise learning to guide your audience toward purchasing. Turning consumers into customers is a process that requires strategy, communication and engagement.

There are many ways to monetise your social media presence, each with its growth potential. Some of the most effective methods include:

+ offering a service
+ selling a product – courses, workshops, templates
+ membership model
+ gartnering with brands
+ platform advertisements.

By leveraging these strategies, you can turn your social media presence into a thriving business and a source of sustainable income.

OFFERING A SERVICE

To sell a service, people must first know what you offer. If you've followed the previous chapters, you will understand the importance of capturing attention, engaging your audience and making your brand memorable. The first step to selling is visibility.

Once visible, the key is presenting your offer to the right people with the right messaging. This is where audience targeting, avatar building, content diversification and a multi-platform strategy are essential. Avoid the 'hire me' or 'buy now' approach, which many architecture firms rely on through polished, hyper-realistic renderings. While these images may look impressive, they function more as portfolio pieces than effective marketing tools and provide no real value to anyone. People hire people, not pictures.

A value-focused strategy is emphasised in 'Marketing for Architects: The Authoritative Guide' by Enoch Sears in *Business of Architecture*. He discusses that the issue with most traditional marketing is that practices only target a tiny portion of their potential audience – about 3% – who are immediately ready to hire an architect. These clients are already in the 'buy now' mindset, a limited group.[2] Most firms rely on this narrow approach, hoping their polished ads or posts will reach someone ready to make a big decision, which is a long shot. Suppose your message only reaches people in the hiring stage. In that case, you're missing out on the large majority (97%) still in the early phases of gathering information, scouting and exploring options.

Sears offers a solution in this article: instead of pushing direct sales, practices should create educational content that appeals to those in the early 'idea gathering' stage.[3] His logic is that by providing valuable resources, you build trust and establish your firm as a knowledgeable authority before a potential client even thinks about hiring. This approach helps develop relationships with future clients, ensuring they know, like and trust your firm when they're ready to move to hire you.

Think about your ideal client – before they hire you, they need to see that you are experienced, capable and trustworthy. Your social media strategy should focus on demonstrating your expertise and building credibility. The best way to achieve this is through valuable, educational content. Share step-by-step guides, behind-the-scenes insights and process breakdowns that showcase your skills. Use eye-catching graphics and informative posts to explain architectural concepts clearly and engagingly. Most importantly, show your personality. By focusing on personability and value, relationship building develops rather than just pushing the final product; you'll find that work naturally follows. Trust and connection are what ultimately convert interest into long-term clients.

SELLING A PRODUCT – COURSES, WORKSHOPS, TEMPLATES

Like selling a service, you may choose to sell your knowledge, which is particularly popular among profiles focused on educational content, as there is a natural connection between the free content shared and the courses or workshops offered as paid products. As viewers engage with your free educational material, providing a deeper level of guidance and education makes a paid product the logical next step. This creates progression in the audience's academic journey with your profile, encouraging a deeper insight into the profile's expertise.

This approach is a rewarding business strategy for both the creator and the customer. The creator benefits financially by monetising their skills and expertise while also experiencing the fulfilment of guiding and helping others. The paid product gives customers access to much deeper, more comprehensive educational material, allowing them to understand better the skill or process they want to master. Additionally, the customer forms a stronger connection with the creator through this more direct learning experience. It makes sense.

Here are some profiles and their products:

PROFILE SPOTLIGHT

SHOW IT BETTER

Steven Rubio's profile at Show it Better is focused on teaching others how to communicate architectural ideas effectively, but his mission runs deeper. It's rooted in his experience of finding architectural education 'dense and cryptic', as he describes it. Steven explains that through his content and courses, he's 'on a mission to revolutionise how architectural education is delivered'.[4]

On this mission, Steven has developed pre-recorded courses that learners can access anytime, making them super convenient. What makes these courses stand out is their length and depth. Unlike short tutorials or quick lessons, they offer a more detailed and comprehensive learning experience. Some examples of Show It Better courses include:

+ 'Animated Diagrams' – 3 hours, 32 lessons
+ 'Realistic Site Plan' – 2 hours, 25 lessons
+ 'Master Sections' – 3 hours, 34 lessons
+ 'Presentation Boards with InDesign' – 4 hours, 40 lessons.

Each course includes:
+ downloadable templates and resources
+ full lifetime access
+ a certificate of completion.

These courses are examples of pre-recorded, one-time payment courses that grant customers lifetime access. This model allows learners to study at their own pace, making it a flexible and convenient option for those who prefer self-directed learning.

Alternatively, live workshops offer real-time engagement, providing an interactive learning experience where participants can ask questions, receive immediate feedback and engage in discussions.

Figure 4.1 Show it Better's 'Animated Architecture' course.

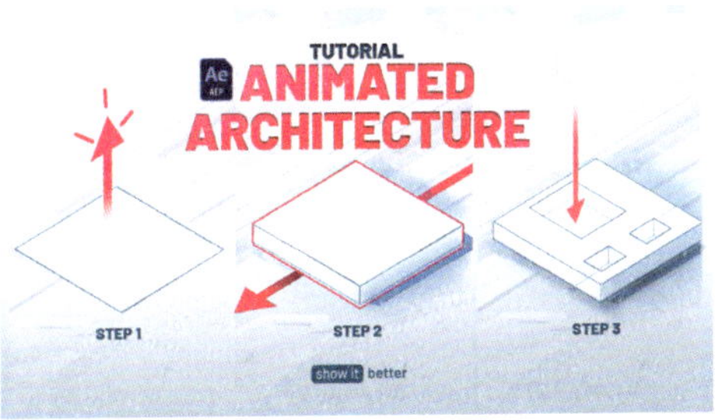

Figure 4.2 Show it Better's general course image.

PROFILE SPOTLIGHT

ARCHITECTURE CANDY

Vishakha Tiwari at Architecture Candy focuses her content on turning followers and consumers from leads into enrolled learners. She runs live workshops on visual design communication, which 'aim to help you articulate your design concepts through compelling graphics, guiding you towards the most effective expression of your ideas'.[5] Vishakha's workshops happen in real time and online.

Some examples of Architecture Candy classes include:
+ 'Massing Diagrams in Architecture' – 3 hours, live
+ 'All About Diagrams' – 6 hours, pre-recorded.

An alternative product that shifts focus from education to efficiency is **templates** – a solution designed to save time and streamline workflows. These products address the pain points of inefficiency by providing ready-made resources that professionals can quickly implement into their projects.

Figure 4.3 Axonometric illustration colour style.

Figure 4.4: Self-paced course on diagrams on Adobe Illustrator.

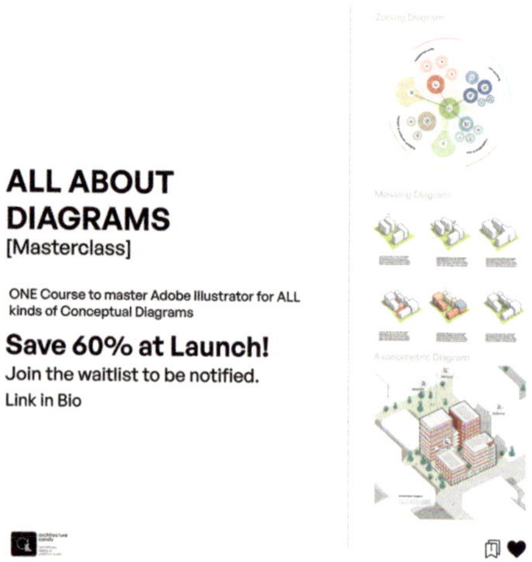

PROFILE SPOTLIGHT

INITIATE ARCHITECTURE

Ross Hartland views his template products as valuable tools his customers can easily implement into their architecture projects:

+ Project Filing System
+ Diagram Toolkit
+ Notion Client Portal
+ AutoCAD Title Block Pack.

These ready-to-use resources offer practical solutions for everyday challenges within architecture, making them highly appealing to customers looking for efficiency and quality in their project processes.

Figure 4.5: Initiate Architecture's Client Portal thumbnail.

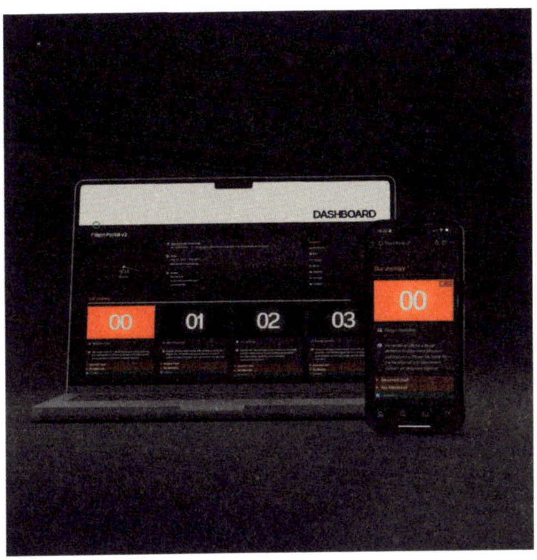

Figure 4.6: Initiate Architecture's Diagram Toolkit thumbnail.

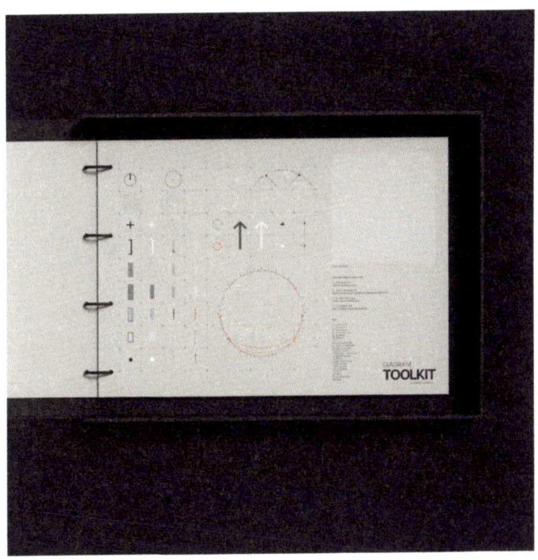

LEAD MAGNET

To sell a product is a journey of turning a consumer into a customer. Whether you have the base of an existing audience or are seeking one, if you intend to sell to your audience, there is a strategy. One discussed by Alex Hormozi in *$100M Leads* is the lead magnet. Fundamentally, a lead is someone you can contact, but an engaged lead is different.[6] When someone provides their contact information, downloads a free resource, signs up for a newsletter or follows you, they actively show interest in what you offer and become an engaged lead. These individuals are more likely to convert into paying customers. A lead magnet is a lower cost or free offer designed to gauge interest in your products or services, similar to a most viable product, a beta version of your main product, aimed as a gateway or entry to your product ecosystem.

The goal of a lead magnet is to engage these interested leads by offering something of value for free, such as a product sample or webinar, preferably involving interested leads in sharing their contact details, particularly their email, demographics and location. Collecting this data allows you to maintain ongoing communication, gauge interest in your services and monitor the level of interest in your services. Understanding your leads' buying patterns and pain points enables you to tailor your offerings to meet their needs better. The more detailed your insights, the more effectively you can create targeted content, nurture relationships and convert leads into paying customers. Simply put, if people find value in your free offer, they invest in the full, paid version. Like Ross's marketing funnel approach in drawing leads to his website, the emphasis is on providing upfront value to build trust and channel interest towards your paid product or services. By showing the worth of your lead magnet, you increase the chances of converting leads into paying customers.

You've likely encountered lead magnets from many businesses and profiles you follow – they're everywhere. A great example of a lead magnet is the Sketching Retreat by David Drazil. It offers immense value upfront, attracting participants with free workshops and content focused on architectural sketching.

PROFILE SPOTLIGHT

SKETCHING RETREAT – DAVID DRAZIL

The Sketching Retreat is a free six-day event, featuring 30 to 50 video workshops on different architectural sketching techniques using various mediums. David says, 'The idea is simple: for a limited time, we create an architectural sketching online summit, like a traditional conference, but virtual.'

He continues, 'When an online summit is done right, they are a win-win-win for everyone involved. It's a win for the attendees, a win for the instructors and a win for me as the organiser. Importantly, the event has a targeted audience: people interested in architectural sketching, whether pen and paper, watercolour or digital techniques.' It's an event with immense value offered at no cost to attendees, but the monetisation comes later from those who want extended access to the workshops. David explains, 'Since the event runs for six days, not everyone has time to view everything during that window. So, we offer a VIP ticket that provides unlimited, on-demand access to all workshops. This VIP ticket also includes bonus content, enhancing its value.'

Figure 4.7 Sketching Retreat banner.

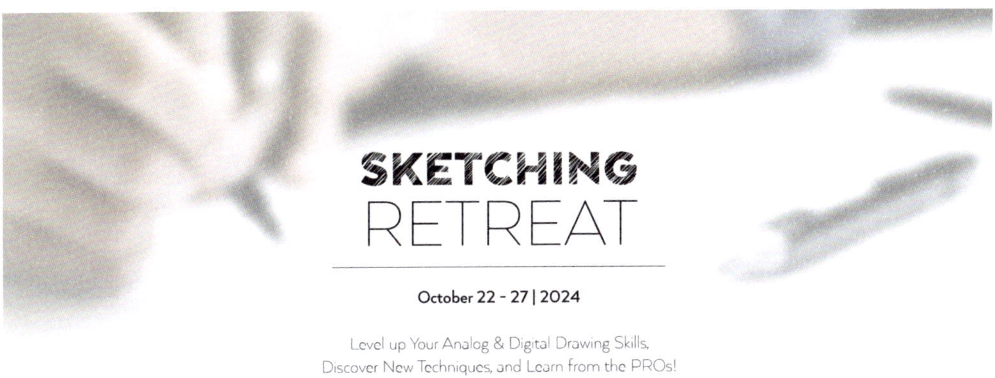

Figure 4.8 Sketching Retreat banner.

Figure 4.9 Sketching Retreat banner, listing the instructors.

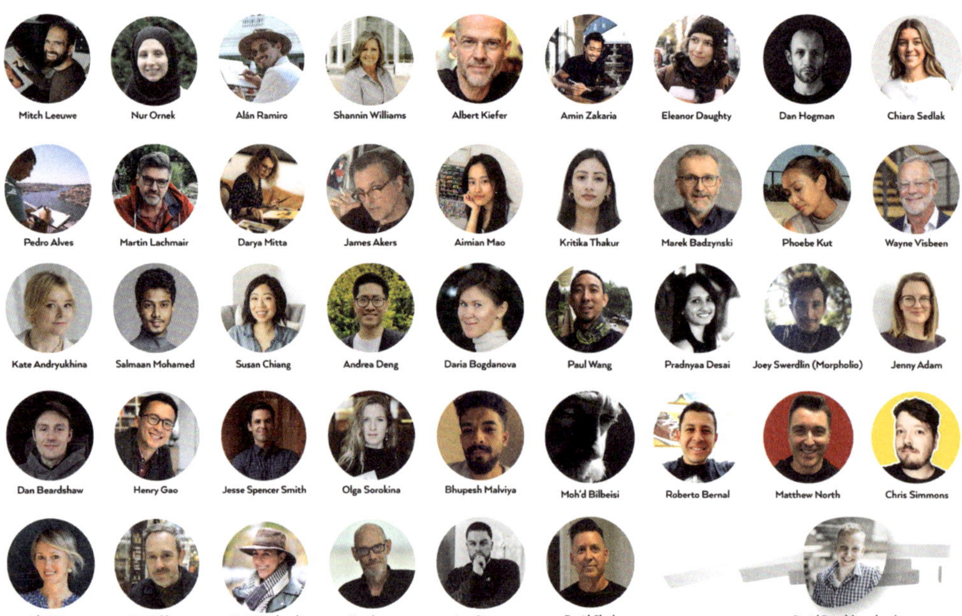

What sets this summit apart from others is the profit-sharing model. 'I don't keep all the profit; 50% of the event's profit is shared with the contributing instructors, and they also benefit from affiliate marketing, where they earn a 50% commission for every VIP ticket sold through their referrals. Furthermore, instructors are encouraged to offer content upgrades or freebies (lead magnets) alongside their workshops to grow their email database. This creates huge value for the instructors, attendees and me. I value this opportunity to network with amazing artists, build relationships and bring new people into my ecosystem. It's much work – I usually prepare for three or four months – but it's worth it.'

For David, the Sketching Retreat draws tens of thousands of sign-ups and thousands of attendees, all gaining immense value while becoming engaged leads by sharing their contact information. This gives him a direct line to potential customers for future product launches, services and events, fostering a long-term connection beyond the initial retreat. It's a prime example of turning leads into engaged leads – and ultimately into paying customers – by first delivering exceptional free value.

BE CRYSTAL CLEAR

One of the most important principles in selling a product is clarity. Hormozi emphasises that if you give your audience any reason to hesitate or doubt, they won't spend their hard-earned money. A confused mind doesn't buy, so your messaging needs to be crystal clear.[7]

Just as a clear and understandable message is vital for forming a strong brand identity and encouraging audience engagement, your product approach must be equally straightforward. If your audience isn't sure what your product is or how it benefits them, they won't engage with it. Each product example from successful creators such as Show it Better, Architecture Candy and Initiate Architecture has clarity and alignment with their content strategy. These products align with their respective content strategies, making it easy for their audiences to understand the value offered.

ACTIONABLE STEP

If you're looking to turn a consumer into a customer, focus on these four components:

1. Clarity
Be clear about what your product offers and how it adds value. Ensure it aligns with your brand message. Focus on your product's visual and verbal communication and speak directly to your audience, making it clear that your product solves their problem. Make the benefits obvious, and the decision to purchase becomes easier.

2. Create a Minimum Viable Product (MVP)
An MVP is a simple version of your product that solves a key problem. It allows you to launch quickly, gather feedback and refine it over time. This helps your audience experience the product's value without a significant upfront investment.

3. Keep a mailing list
Provide free, valuable content and build trust through a mailing list. Email newsletters deepen relationships and keep your audience updated on new products or promotions, creating long-term engagement.

4. Use Call to Action (CTA)
Guide your audience on what to do next with clear CTAs, whether signing up for a newsletter, downloading a resource or purchasing. A CTA could be anything from 'Click the link in the video description', 'Comment "Archi" to join the newsletter', 'Subscribe today for more content' or 'Swipe up to learn more'. A strong CTA directs your audience to taking action without any friction.

In summary, success lies in clear messaging, creating an MVP, building relationships with a mailing list and using effective CTAs. These strategies connect your content and product, making it easier for your audience to engage and take the next step. Start today and ensure your product aligns with your brand's value.

MEMBERSHIP MODEL

The value of the membership model lies in its ability to offer members something unique and valuable that they can't get elsewhere – this model is based on exclusivity. A membership platform can include exclusivity to content, community access, or product or service discounts. Much of the value for the member lies in a sense of belonging, where individuals feel connected to a group of like-minded people who share their interests or goals – a deeper and more closely connected space than social media where the members can speak amongst themselves or with the educator/s or creator/s.

Membership is often hidden behind a paywall, and the member must pay a recurring monthly or annual fee to access it. This is similar to the subscription-based model with Netflix, Disney+ or Paramount+. The member pays a fee and, in return, gains access to the material offered in the membership.

Typically, there are four main types of membership models:

1. **Exclusive content:** Members gain access to exclusive content such as tutorials, videos or blog posts – depending on the intended focus of the content – that is typically educational and/or behind-the-scenes content not available on other social platforms. This type of content could be in the form of a library or scheduled in a drip-content format, similar to a weekly TV show.
2. **Networking and community:** This model allows members to join a community of people with similar interests, providing networking opportunities, group discussions and collaborations.
3. **Exclusive access to products or services at a discount:** Members enjoy special offers or discounts on products or services, giving them financial perks to their membership.
4. **Bundled memberships:** This combines several benefits – like exclusive content, community access and discounts – into one comprehensive package, providing more value for the membership fee.

Take the ArchAdemia membership as an example.

PROFILE SPOTLIGHT

COURSE LIBRARY – ARCHADEMIA

ArchAdemia is a leading membership platform for the architecture community, offering a comprehensive range of educational resources. As explained by Adam Morgan, ArchAdemia's co-founder, the platform was created to give 'students, graduates and young practitioners a place where they could ask "silly questions" confidently, learn key skills not covered in university or the early stages of their career and foster a sense of community.'

Its membership operates on a bundled model with exclusive content and valuable community benefits. At its core, ArchAdemia is a course provider, and it has developed a wide range of content with a team of eight specialists, including architects, BIM managers and 3D artists. It currently offers:

+ **50 courses** that cover everything needed to launch any educational or professional career in the construction industry.

Figure 4.10 A typical ArchAdemia course dashboard.

Figure 4.11 Preview of ArchAdemia members' area.

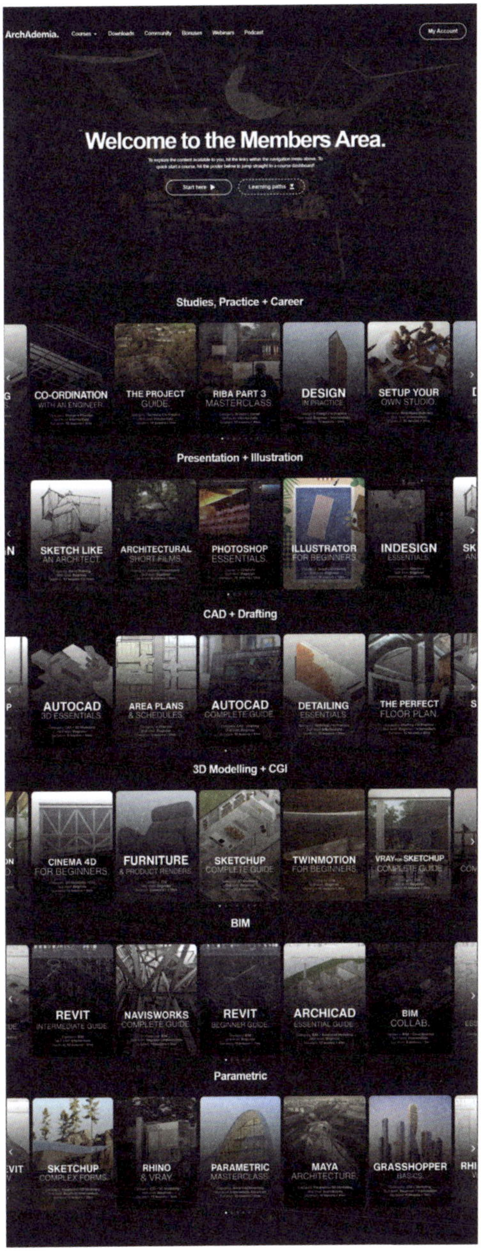

+ **Member bonuses**, which include additional lessons and downloadable content.
+ **A community forum** where members can interact with each other and the tutors.
+ **20 downloadable packs**, which offer templates and frameworks for essential areas like planning applications, Revit models, filing systems, project management, etc.
+ **One-on-one support on request**, along with a monthly webinar where members can submit content requests through a newsletter.

ArchAdemia uses the Kajabi platform to host its courses, praising its advanced infrastructure for educational content. ArchAdemia initially used Squarespace for its storefront but outgrew its capabilities after a year, citing limitations such as a page cap and a lack of search functionality. To improve the user experience and site performance, it transitioned to WordPress, offering better Search Engine Optimisation (SEO) capabilities and a more refined customer journey.

The membership platform is central to ArchAdemia's business model, providing a sustainable source of income. It offers subscriptions through either a monthly or annual fee. Significantly, it has adjusted its pricing based on market feedback, ensuring it remains affordable for students and those not working full time.

This membership model has proven to be its primary means of monetisation, especially compared to revenue streams like YouTube or TikTok. As explained, 'Payments from social platforms like YouTube and TikTok are much lower than expected, with platforms taking a significant cut. Directing our audience to our platform has been a far more effective way to generate income and control the process.'

Moreover, the membership model doesn't just support ArchAdemia – it also helps fund its architecture practice, Studio RBA. This model provides 'a steady, more predictable income than relying on social platforms or running an architecture practice, where cash flow can be a major challenge'. While Studio RBA projects may bring in more considerable fees, the unpredictable nature of architecture work, including project delays and economic fluctuations, means that ArchAdemia provides crucial financial stability for the practice.

ArchAdemia is a powerful example of how an architecture practice can diversify its income streams through social media – specifically by leveraging education and industry insights. While creating a platform of this scale may seem unattainable for many firms, it highlights the vast monetary potential of using social media to sell knowledge, expertise and experience – all of which architecture practices already possess in abundance.

PARTNERING WITH BRANDS

Often referred to as 'brand deals' or 'brand collaborations', these partnerships have arisen due to the exposure and engagement content creators can garner. Simply put, a brand partnership involves an agreement between two parties (typically creator and brand) where the creator shares one or more pieces of content to promote and endorse a product or service. This is also known as influencer marketing.

The goal is for the brand to tap into the creator's established audience and engagement, gain access to a specific demographic that aligns with the brand's target market, and raise awareness of a brand's product, service and message.

A brand partnership may strike through various methods:

+ **brand outreach to the creator** – contact through email, direct message
+ **creator outreach to the brand** – contact through email, direct message
+ **agencies** – intermediatory communication between creator and brand.

Influencer marketing is no joke and has skyrocketed over the past decade, becoming a major force in digital advertising. The industry's estimated market size for 2024 has surged to $24 billion, an impressive rise from $1.4 billion in 2014.[8] Brands are investing heavily to tap into creators' audiences, recognising the value of authentic engagement and the benefits that are mutual.

Brand Benefit

For brands, the primary goal of a brand deal is to reach new but highly relevant audiences and leverage the creator's influence to build trust and recognition with their message or product. The creator's audience has already formed a connection with the content creator, so when a brand collaborates with them, it creates an organic connection that traditional advertising often lacks.

As Ben Zimmerman, former president at Media Design Group, states in 'The Importance of Authenticity And Loyalty In Brand Partnerships', 'The key here isn't the creative or the ad itself. It's the partnership that truly matters.' He adds, 'They're providing the content that their audience already wants. They've already hooked them – it's a matter of delivery at this point. As the advertiser, you're simply connecting the dots for them and overlaying their content with your data-driven insight to reach viewers on channels that have the most reach.'[9]

Creator Benefit

For creators, their reach and engaged audience are incredibly valuable assets to brands, making brand partnerships a lucrative opportunity. Brands are often willing to compensate creators, offering flat fees, commissions or even products as payment. For example, a brand might provide £1,500 per content in exchange for the creator reviewing it in a YouTube video. This form of compensation is a key aspect of the partnership, ensuring the creator is rewarded for their influence and effort.

Beyond immediate financial gains, an additional incentive for creators to collaborate with brands is the potential for building long-term partnerships, which provides creators with financial stability while fostering a stronger alliance built on trust. This relationship often grants greater creative flexibility, allowing creators to integrate brand promotions in a way that stays authentic to their audience while still delivering effective advertising. This authenticity leads to a stronger connection between the audience and the brand, which can boost product sales or increase clickthrough rates. This can result in higher commissions and better compensation over time for the creator.

AUTHENTIC BRAND PARTNERSHIPS

A crucial aspect of successful brand deals is the alignment between the brand, the creator and the creator's audience. The partnership must make sense for both parties and resonate with the creator's audience. For example, tomrowstudios frequently collaborates with architectural drawing and modelling software brands, focusing on improving drawing workflows and efficiency. This fits perfectly with my content, which revolves around educating designers on streamlining their workflows and enhancing their presentation skills. The alignment is transparent and authentic, making the partnership a natural extension of my brand.

On the other hand, a collaboration with a brand like Coca-Cola or Nike, while exciting, would feel out of place. Since those products don't align with the architecture documentation style content, it could lead to confusion or scepticism from my audience, who might question why I chose to partner with such brands. Misalignment like this could dilute the authenticity of a creator's platform.

Rishabh Wadhwa from Blessedarch shares a similar approach to brand partnerships, ensuring the brands he works with align with the Blessedarch message. He explains, 'For Instagram, I integrate branded content within my regular posts, making it seem natural and not overly promotional. I prefer integrated videos where the brand is a part of the content rather than dedicated advertisements on YouTube.'

Rishabh also emphasises the importance of building strong relationships with brands. 'Brands usually reach out to me through intermediaries, but I also proactively contact brands I want to work with. Building relationships with brands involves creating good content and delivering results, leading to repeat collaborations.'

Social media content creators and influencers are incredibly attractive for brands looking to advertise. If you have a targeted, engaged audience in a specific niche, brands will pay to have their products endorsed by you. If your social media presence showcases an expertise or impressive portfolio of work, you'll be in the spotlight for potential clients and collaborators.

PLATFORM ADVERTISEMENTS

While much of the focus on monetising your social media profile involves brand partnerships, selling your products, or using social media as a lead magnet for memberships, courses or workshops, there's also a way to be directly compensated by the platforms. Platforms like YouTube, Instagram, Facebook, TikTok and Snapchat all offer creators a share of the revenue through ads that run alongside their content.

Here's how it works: businesses pay to place ads on these platforms, to reach specific audiences based on demographics, interests, viewing habits and behaviours. These ads help brands target their ideal customers more effectively. For example, on YouTube, advertisements may play before, during or after a video. Some ads are skippable, while others aren't, but even a skippable 30-second ad can make an impact in just the first 5 seconds. That brief exposure is often enough to get viewers interested, or at least aware of the product.

Earning through ad revenue share programs, such as those offered by YouTube and TikTok, has become the second most common monetisation method for creators, only behind live streaming in 2024, according to research by Epidemic Sound, which surveyed 1,500 monetising creators.[10] YouTube is the top social platform for generating income in 2024.

Using YouTube as the primary example, creators can join the YouTube Partner Program once their channel reaches 1,000 subscribers and accumulates 4,000 watch hours within 12 months. This means that monetisation doesn't happen immediately after starting a channel. It takes time and consistent content creation before a creator can start earning through their earning program – AdSense. The amount of revenue a creator earns is influenced by several factors, such as:

+ the number of viewers on a video
+ the watch hours – how long people stay engaged with the video
+ viewer interaction with ads, such as clicks or engagement with ad content.

Generally, more views increase earnings because more people are exposed to the ads. However, it's not just about views – video length and retention rates also play significant roles. For example, a 30-minute video with strong retention (around 45%) and multiple ads spaced throughout can generate more revenue than a shorter video with the same number of views. This is

Figure 4.12 Thomas Rowntree, 'A Day in the Life of an Architecture Student' thumbnail.

because the longer video offers more opportunities for viewers to see and engage with multiple ads, increasing the chances of earning a higher payout.

To give you an idea of how revenue is shared, and for complete transparency, the top two highest-viewed videos (at the time of writing) on the Thomas Rowntree YouTube channel are:

+ 'A Day in the Life of an Architecture Student' – 229,600 views
+ 'Best Laptop for Architecture. How to Choose your Laptop for Architecture' – 100,400 views

They each earned, respectively:

+ £431.03
+ £332.39

and continue to earn passively.

While two of the videos reached over 90,000 views, with one surpassing 225,000, the average views per video typically hovers around the 10,000 mark.

Figure 4.13: Thomas Rowntree, 'A Day in the Life of an Architecture Student' analytics.

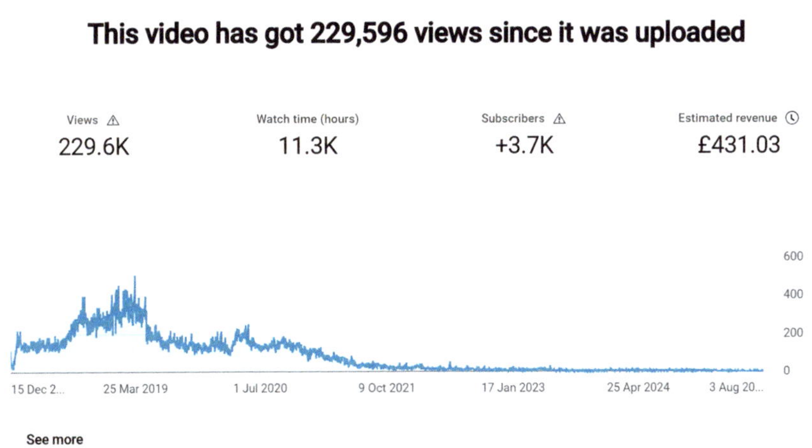

This translates to earning roughly £25 per video – not enough to sustain a YouTube channel long term. This reality is why many creators venture into brand partnerships and develop their products, as these avenues offer the potential for significantly higher income.

The actual earning power from YouTube advertisement monetisation comes when you consistently hit 100,000+ views per video. This can be seen with creators such as Dami Lee, 30X40 Design Workshop, Show it Better and Upstairs, to name a few. The financial rewards through ad revenue can be substantial for creators who can achieve that reach. However, for many creators, reaching those numbers regularly is a challenge. This gap in consistent high viewership pushes creators to diversify their income streams beyond just YouTube ad revenue, tapping into more reliable and profitable methods like brand deals and product sales.

Figure 4.14: Thomas Rowntree, 'Best Laptop for Architecture. How to Choose your Laptop for Architecture' thumbnail.

Monetising your brand through social media offers a wealth of opportunities to boost product sales, expand your client portfolio and generate sustainable income. By leveraging various strategies – selling products, offering services, creating educational content or partnering with brands – your social media presence can become a powerful tool for financial success. Authenticity and clear communication are key to building trust with your audience; essential for converting followers into paying customers. Whether an individual creator or a business, a well-executed social media strategy can unlock new revenue streams and significantly expand your reach.

Figure 4.15: Thomas Rowntree, 'Best Laptop for Architecture. How to Choose Your Laptop for Architecture' analytics.

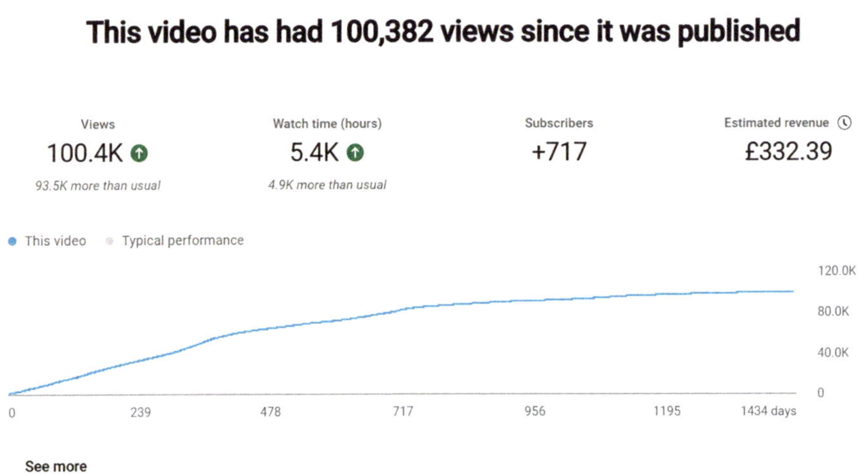

A CONVERSATION WITH
DAVID DRAZIL
SKETCH LIKE AN ARCHITECT

David Drazil, founder of Sketch Like an Architect, helps architects, designers, and hobby sketchers become confident in their traditional and digital drawing skills to communicate their ideas and observations more effectively.

In my conversation with David Drazil, creator of the successful Sketching Retreat and various products, I sought to learn more about his product development approach. We discussed how he aligns his product creation with his brand message and identity, and the strategies behind building his suite of products.

Thomas: *I'd love to hear more about your journey in content creation. At what point did you decide to start creating and selling products? Did you always intend to use social media as a business tool, or did that develop later?*

David: It all started while studying for my master's in architecture at Aalborg University in Denmark. I was in a diverse environment with students from all over Europe, and I noticed a big difference in presentation skills. Some students created beautiful, clear presentations, while others struggled to communicate their ideas visually. The key difference seemed to be whether they had taken drawing courses during their bachelor's studies. In Denmark, there was only one optional semester for observational drawing, whereas students from countries like Poland or the Czech Republic had multiple semesters of technical and artistic drawing.

I realised that those drawing skills transferred to all kinds of visual communication, whether it was sketching, diagrams or digital presentations. However, not everyone had the chance to develop those skills. That was the gap I identified. After graduating, I was unemployed for a while, doing volunteer work and consuming a lot of online courses. It struck me that I could offer something similar – a basic architectural sketching course for those without formal drawing training.

At the time, I also wanted to build an online presence to help with job applications, but creating a website seemed too complicated. Instagram was much easier, so I started there, sharing my work and educational content on sketching. I had no experience in marketing or online courses, so I was learning as I went. My first course, 'Sketch Like an Architect', came together as I experimented with content on Instagram.

Thomas: *It's fascinating to hear how your personal experience inspired the course. Many creators start their social media journey by addressing gaps they've experienced firsthand. How did you go about creating that first course?*

David: It was all pre-recorded, but looking back, I made some mistakes. The biggest one was not validating the idea before putting in the work. I spent six months developing the course without knowing if people would actually want it. I had assumptions, but no solid feedback. Luckily, it worked out, but it was risky. If I could do it again, I'd test the idea first to make sure there was interest. Despite that, taking action and making mistakes taught me a lot. Over time, I developed a clearer understanding of what my audience needed.

Thomas: *You've certainly learned from that experience. Now, you offer a variety of products at different price points and skill levels. How important has it been to offer different options for your audience?*

David: Many highly successful businesses focus on just one or two big products, and that's enough. In my case, I have around 20 different products, most of them smaller, which build up what's called a product ladder or an ascension model. But that's largely the result of experimenting and testing what works to satisfy the needs of my audience. For example, in my 'Sketch Like an Architect' ecosystem, I don't just offer digital products and courses. There are also eBooks, physical books, one-on-one teaching and even in-person workshops here in Prague. I've had the chance to speak at universities too. The ecosystem evolves as I do – what I enjoy creating changes over time, and I adjust it to suit my preferences and needs. Looking back, I've learned that focusing on one specific product or problem that's significant enough to solve for your audience is often a more straightforward path to success – too many options can overwhelm people. Lately, I've been focusing on simplifying things. I've learned that clarity is essential, both for me and for my audience. If you spread yourself too thin, it's harder to maintain quality and manage the back end of the business.

05
DEVELOPING ORGANISATION RECOGNITION

+ A Conversation with Oliver Thomas

At the time of writing, the architecture content creation space is still in its infancy. The profiles you see in this book represent a small but growing group of individuals who have recognised the value of social media, while the majority of the architecture profession seems slow to catch on. Whether it's due to the profession's tendency to be slow in adopting new trends or a lack of understanding and precedent in the space, many practices have yet to grasp the potential of these platforms.

In this chapter, we will explore practice-specific strategies for communicating value, leveraging social media as a networking tool and capturing the attention of your ideal audience. While many core principles – such as unique selling proposition (USP), niching, storytelling and conversation-building – have been discussed earlier, this section will focus on how to apply them effectively from a practice perspective. You'll learn how to position your practice, engage with potential clients and collaborators, and use social media to strengthen your brand and business opportunities. If you work within an architecture practice and have any influence over marketing strategies, it's time to reconsider your approach.

BUCKING THE TREND

As discussed in Chapter 4: Monetisation and Entrepreneurship, while discussing offering a service, currently, the most common approach by architecture practices on social media is to recycle final CGIs, drawings or marketing photography from their websites, award submissions or other marketing channels. Often, these posts are paired with generic captions like 'We are pleased to announce that [insert project name] has won/been nominated for [insert award name]'. Sound familiar? This approach misses the mark. While this might work to some extent on LinkedIn, where professionals are more inclined to see industry updates, it's not catching any trends or engaging wider audiences.

What's being missed is the opportunity to showcase the components of an architecture practice that genuinely resonate with people: the individuals behind the designs, office culture, design and drawing processes, emotion, experience and all the human side of architecture. In today's social media age, people are tired of seeing only final renders and polished photography. These posts lack substance, story, authenticity and, most importantly, value. They don't engage architects, let alone the average consumer.

As an experienced architect, deeply involved in the architecture industry, and having successfully developed his brand, Chris Simmons affirms this position and offers a holistic perspective. He states, 'Architects have been slow to react to social media marketing and the wealth of opportunities for those who embrace it at a low cost and low barrier to entry. Practices need to focus on telling stories, talking about all aspects of their work and process, not just the completed project.' This kind of content, especially in video format, is far more engaging and helps audiences connect with the work on a more personal level. 'The real value lies in storytelling,' Chris affirms.

TIME VS REWARD

The time-to-reward ratio in social media can feel skewed. While building an audience takes time, reaching one can happen instantly. Just as attending a networking event might seem time-consuming, a chance encounter could lead to a long-term client. Social media accelerates this process, simultaneously putting you in multiple rooms worldwide. It's a global networking event, a conference and a conversation starter – all in one.

Take the story of Wojciech Kumik, who told his story on the 30X40 Design Workshop YouTube channel in a video titled 'How this Architect 4X'd His income'. Wojciech graduated in 2017 and worked for several architecture practices before realising the traditional path wasn't for him. He transitioned into a Revit CAD technician role but still had a deep passion for design and architecture. His breakthrough came unexpectedly when an opportunity arose to design a sauna for his parents.[1]

What started as a small family project quickly became something more. Wojciech approached it with the same level of detail as any professional project – creating plans, sections, elevations, renders and construction details. After completing the design, he shared it in a sauna-focused

Facebook group. The response was overwhelming – many members were interested in his design, validating his idea. Wojciech documented the process as he and his father built the sauna, noting improvements and refining the design. He then transformed his work into a sellable product – a PDF package containing drawings, details, schedules and lessons learned from the build.[2] If you're interested in learning more about selling products online, refer to Chapter 4: Monetisation and Entrepreneurship for a deeper dive into the process. He started making sales by leveraging social media and targeting an audience already interested in saunas.

What began as a small side hustle alongside his full-time job quickly grew. Encouraged by early success, he gradually increased his prices and refined his offering. Over time, this passion project evolved into a full-fledged business, allowing Wojciech to earn four times his previous corporate salary and achieve creative independence.[3] His journey highlights the power of social media as a tool for validation, audience engagement and business growth. By sharing his expertise, documenting his process and providing value to a niche audience, Wojciech turned a single project into a profitable and fulfilling career.

Wojciech is one of many success stories of architects and designers who have harnessed social media to find creative freedom and build thriving businesses on their terms. In this book, we have highlighted similar stories from Ross Hartland, a thriving solo practitioner, to Ana Aragão, an architect and illustrator, to the POoR Collective, a community-focused group making an immense impact on communities.

At a larger practice scale, a significant value lies in the networking potential. Take recruitment as an example. A top third-year architecture student skilled in visual communication and award-winning presentations has followed your practice for years, inspired by your design philosophy and culture. When they graduate, your practice is their first choice. Similarly, an experienced architect specialising in high-end hotels is looking for a new challenge. Your social presence has intrigued them, and they reach out, eager to join your team. Attracting top talent strengthens your practice, raising the quality of your work and reputation.

On the client side, a developer scrolling social media sees an image you posted, follows your page and becomes familiar with your expertise. Your practice is high up on their lists when they need an architect. Without direct outreach, you've positioned yourself as their preferred choice through strategic content and engagement. By sharing authentic, value-driven content, you can cultivate relationships with future clients, employees and collaborators long before an opportunity arises. This proactive approach opens doors, builds trust and positions you at the forefront of potential opportunities months or even years in advance.

Your content strategy should align with your available time and resources. Investing in the necessary skills and effort is essential if you aim for high-production content. If resources are limited, a sustainable and efficient content approach will help maintain consistency without overextending yourself.

While social media may not provide immediate financial returns, its long-term value is undeniable. Success requires persistence, patience and strategy – but once cultivated, your audience becomes a powerful asset for business growth and opportunity.

PRACTICE OPPORTUNITIES

There is a myriad of opportunities that come with practising social media correctly.

1. **Build brand recognition**
   Social media helps establish and reinforce your practice's reputation and image. It allows your audience to instantly recognise and associate your work with your values and design philosophy.

2. **Increase exposure**
   By maintaining an active presence on social platforms, your practice can reach more people, whether it's potential clients, collaborators or individuals interested in architecture and design. It's a way to be seen by a wider audience than traditional marketing alone might allow.

3. **Share values and identity**
   Social media allows you to communicate what your practice stands for. You can share not only your projects but also your office culture, your design process and the core values that guide your work. This helps people connect with your brand on a deeper level.

4. **Showcase your work**
   Whether through photography, sketches or videos, social media lets you keep an ongoing record of your practice's work. It's a platform to highlight your design style, innovation and progress, which helps keep your audience engaged and informed about your latest projects.

5. **Talent acquisition**
   More than ever, current and future architects and designers are looking to social media for inspiration and job opportunities. People want to work for practices that align with their values and offer an environment in which they can grow. By showcasing your culture and how you work, you can attract talent that aligns with your practice beliefs, expertise and ambition.

6. **Expand your network**
   Social media is also a great way to build relationships within the industry. Whether connecting with potential clients, collaborators or other architects, an active social media presence can help expand your practice's professional network and open the door to new opportunities.

Whether your goal is to target industry professionals, collaborators, potential clients, future employees or the general public, the goal remains the same: to communicate your values, what you do, how you do it, and showcase your people and expertise. This is all done to build a meaningful relationship with one or more of these target groups. By sharing these elements, you create a narrative that fosters trust, engagement and interest, ultimately leading to stronger connections and opportunities within the industry.

The following examples highlight practices of different scales that have embraced social media as a primary marketing strategy and reaped the benefits. Despite their differences, they share three core components that drive engagement and success:

1. **Value**
   They provide educational or insightful content that resonates with their audience.
2. **People**
   They showcase the individuals behind the work, making their brand more relatable and human.
3. **Process**
   They document the journey, sharing behind-the-scenes insights, challenges and creative workflows.

These practices have transformed their online presence into a powerful tool for growth, connection, and opportunity by focusing on these elements.

PROFILE SPOTLIGHT

INITIATE ARCHITECTURE - ROSS HARTLAND

Solo practitioner Ross Hartland, founder of Initiate Architecture, has found much success in his social media marketing efforts, expanding his reach, building his network, increasing work exposure and, most importantly, communicating value. Refer to Chapter 1: Building a Personal Brand for Ross's personal brand profile. Ross explains, 'As architects, we struggle to communicate our value to clients over and above the services of architectural designers, draughtspeople and freelancers. Our social media presence often alienates us from the public with copy aimed at impressing our peers and project images, capturing nothing of the exciting, collaborative and personal process that has led to their creation.'

SHARE VALUE

Ross focuses on educating his audience by taking them behind the scenes of his practice. He doesn't just showcase finished projects; he shares the entire process, from sketching ideas to problem-solving on-site. Ross found that static images of projects weren't enough to stand out. Instead, he pivoted to creating content that provided more for his audience: 'Gone were the static images of projects, replaced with dynamic short-form videos and engaging carousels focused on process, workflows, ideas, and lessons.' By educating the public, sharing insights and giving people a peek behind the curtain, he shows the value of what he does and how he does it. 'My objective was clear: provide great value for free, educate the public on the architectural profession, drive engagement, build an audience and organically guide them towards our website.' He's not just promoting himself – he's providing valuable knowledge and sharing experiences. This approach helps potential clients and followers see him not just as an architect but as someone who adds value through his expertise.

DEMONSTRATE VALUE

The second part of Ross's strategy is about making sure his audience, especially potential clients, understand the unique value he and the architect's role bring to the table. It's not just about his services but also his personality, expertise, experience and thoughtful approach to each project. For Ross, 'The most profound lesson I've learned with Initiate is that people invest in people. Yet, architects – including my former self – often use social media to post project photos and marketing copy aimed at peers rather than connecting with clients.' He elaborates, 'Larger-scale practices have a different agenda from small studios; they are large teams working with commercial clients, where capacity, insurance levels, risk avoidance and previous experience are prioritised over the individual. However, in my experience, this approach does not work for a solo architect looking to sell services to the public in a saturated market of other architects, architectural designers and freelancers.

Figure 5.1 A double-storey gable entry with gallery – co-work.

'Any architect knows the challenges of taking a project from concept to completion, navigating budgets, regulations and endless emails. It's understandable to want to share photos of that hard-earned success. But what I've realised is that different platforms serve different purposes. Websites are perfect for showcasing curated portfolios, but Instagram offers a unique opportunity for connection.

'Thanks to algorithms and engaging content, my work, thoughts and lessons as a solo architect from Wales can reach a local, national and global audience. Once I recognised this, Initiate's content became successful. I shifted from just sharing portfolio pieces to sharing my face, personality and the process behind my work. The algorithm favoured short-form videos and carousels, so I began using them to show how I conduct site analysis, feasibility studies, planning packages, and more. This approach allowed me to connect more deeply with my audience.'

Figure 5.2 Enscape architectural render.

'MARKETING WHEEL'

Finally, Ross uses his strategy to channel people genuinely interested in what he's sharing into his practice's 'hub' – a lead magnet strategy. He talks of this strategy as the 'Marketing Wheel' concept. In this model, the website is the central hub, and the social media and other marketing tools act as spokes to drive traffic back to it. Ross generates real interest in his work by first building a relationship and guiding his audience toward his practice – it's a way to naturally funnel those who appreciate his lessons, knowledge and personal approach into future collaborations or projects. He explains, 'It felt perverse to use social media as a "copy and paste" of the content that already existed on my website; this offers nothing unique, engaging or exciting. Instead, I began a journey to leverage the unique value of social media's powerful algorithms to maximise reach and drive traffic to my website.'

Figure 5.3 An art gallery front – night visualisation.

Figure 5.4 Title block thumbnail – product.

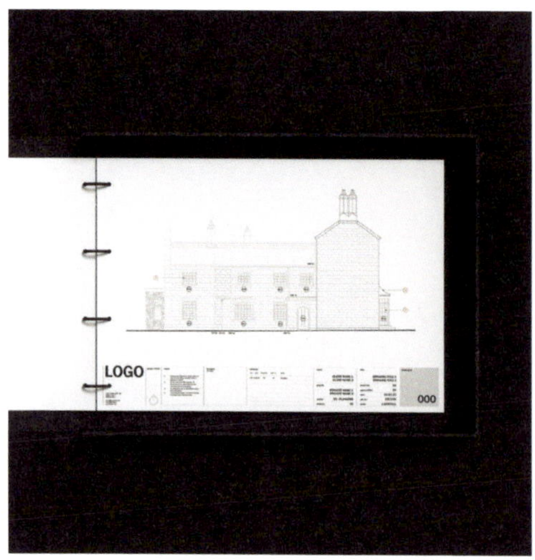

PROFILE SPOTLIGHT

GEMMA WHEELER – YOUTUBE

Gemma Wheeler, an architect dedicated to designing thoughtful and beautiful homes, has built a strong presence on YouTube through her channel, Gemma Wheeler Architecture. Her content focuses on transforming worn and neglected buildings into functional, bespoke tiny homes. Through a combination of design tools and communication techniques, she problem-solves her way to stunning, practical renovations.

Gemma captivates her audience with meticulous and insightful explanations, guiding viewers through each step of her design process. Her videos typically include:

+ project brief and existing building analysis: showcasing images, videos, mood boards and material palettes
+ CGI and walkthroughs of the existing space: helping visualise current conditions
+ sketches and design proposals: discussing layouts, materials and details
+ digital 3D modelling walkthroughs: exploring form, structure and lighting
+ final CGI and proposal walkthroughs: presenting a realistic visualisation of materiality, lighting and furniture
+ voice-over narration: providing detailed design insights.

What makes Gemma's videos so insightful and engaging is her ability to seamlessly weave together various design and communication tools into a curated, narrated journey. She stitches together sketches, CGI, photography and walkthroughs, making her storytelling engaging, clear and easy to follow. This thoughtful presentation showcases her expertise and serves as a subtle marketing tool, demonstrating the value of her design process to potential clients.

Beyond YouTube, Gemma offers one-to-one consultations, helping clients refine their floorplans and sketch ideas. She also provides full design concept services for architectural stages 1 and 2, mirroring the process seen in her videos – effectively turning content into a powerful lead-generation tool.

At the micro-scale practices of Initiate Architecture and Gemma Wheeler Architecture, demonstrating expertise and value has been key to selling architectural services. Using their platforms as a gateway into their offerings, they have effectively turned social media into a client funnel.

Beyond showcasing their work, their educational and insightful approach has resonated with a mass audience, cultivating the support of hundreds of thousands of engaged followers willing to engage and share their skills with friends and family – a perfect storm for building a portfolio of work and gaining a sustainable workstream as a solo practitioner.

SORDO MADALENO

Sordo Madaleno is an interdisciplinary architecture, urban and interior design firm dedicated to creating human-centred environments for the last 87 years.

SOCIAL PLATFORMS

+ INSTAGRAM
  @sordo_madaleno
+ LINKEDIN
  Sordo Madaleno

CONTENT TYPES

+ Short-form video (10-60 seconds)
+ Image carousels

MESSAGE

Sordo Madaleno, an architecture, urban and interior design firm based in Mexico City and London, and dedicated to creating human-centred environments, has nearly 90 years of experience and a broad portfolio exploring typology, context and scale. 'Our sensitivity to context differentiates us and fosters a sense of ownership and belonging in our architecture. Research and a deep understanding of context inform our design decisions throughout our creative process and methodology. We create systems that dialogue with the natural, cultural and built

Figure 5.5 Conceptual sketch of Akumal Monterrey, San Pedro Garza García, Nuevo León, Mexico, 2024.

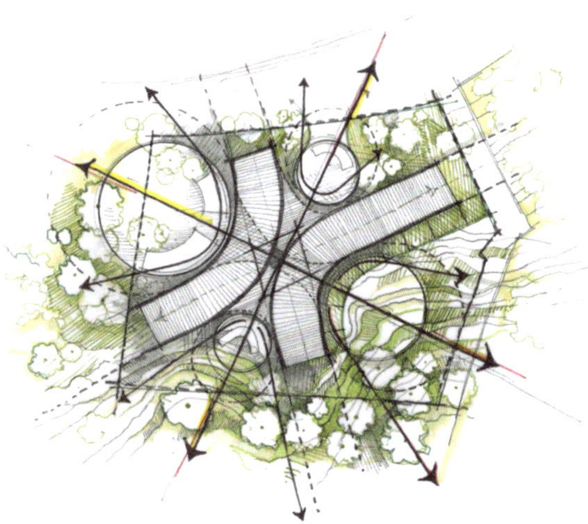

environments. A project may begin with a simple sketch and evolve in many ways.'

A practice with a rich history and portfolio embraces social media as a documentation tool to share its message. 'Sordo Madaleno's central message on social media is to openly communicate the design process behind our projects. We document the process; it provides a complete narrative. Documenting and sharing the creative process is key to our communication strategy. Social media helps a lot with our digital approach, serving as a tool that reflects our practice's daily life and processes. We believe that sharing this intimate process rooted in knowledge and experience opens a window into the studio and allows us to connect with people creatively and empathetically. We see social media as a highly effective tool for building and contributing to collective knowledge and ideas. We are committed to bringing a source of both information and inspiration.

Figure 5.6 Diagram of Akumal Monterrey, San Pedro Garza García, Nuevo León, Mexico, 2024.

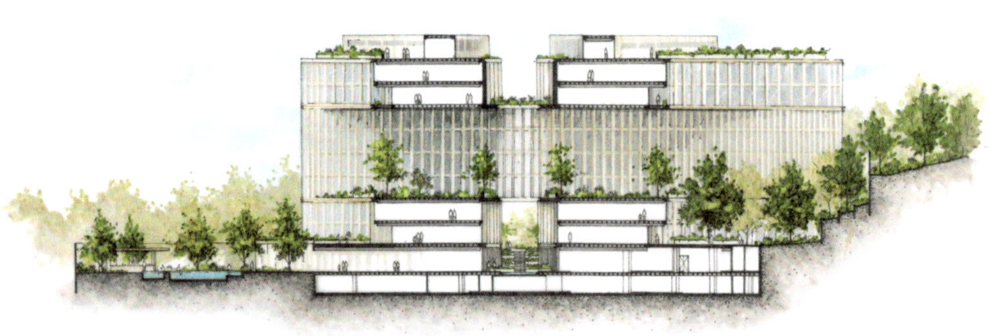

Social media is integral to how we communicate our philosophy and practice. Not only has it helped us grow as a practice, but it has also allowed us to maintain our essence by communicating in a dynamic, transparent and authentic manner.'

STRATEGY

Sharing the Process

Sordo Madaleno's social media approach stems from its openness to share its journey. It has taken a transparent approach, inviting its audience as observant into the heart of its creative process and practice. As explained, 'Our content strategy, developed by our Communication Team, focuses on clearly and carefully communicating processes through information gathering and ongoing documentation of each

Figure 5.7 Akumal Monterrey, San Pedro Garza García, Nuevo León, Mexico, 2024.

design phase: strategic, conceptual, under construction and completed. We work closely with various areas of the firm to build a narrative that spans from project conception to understanding the site, its context, construction challenges and its current and future needs.'

This transparency isn't just about showcasing finished projects – it's about sharing the before, during and after, taking the viewer on the project's journey over time. 'In addition to projects, we share the daily life of the office through audiovisuals, including site visits, processes, news about internal events, lectures, awards and publications.' Such willingness to share the process and design thinking has garnered audience attention, who are interested in the real-life design process. Sordo Madaleno fosters a deeper understanding of its craft and people by presenting its work and process through a mix of visuals, writing and other techniques.

Figure 5.8 Conceptual sketch for Bodegas del Viento Winery, Arteaga, Coahuila, Mexico, 2024.

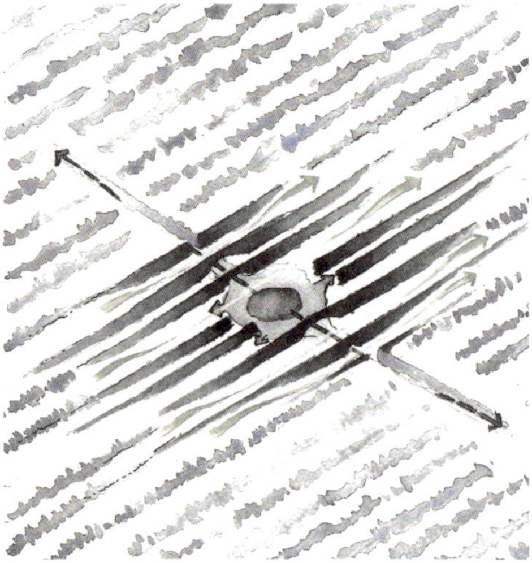

Figure 5.9 Process sketch for Bodegas del Viento Winery, Arteaga, Coahuila, Mexico, 2024.

Content Variety

Sordo Madaleno uses a tailored, multi-platform strategy to effectively share its process and culture. It adapts its content to suit each platform's audience and format. 'On Instagram, our profile is primarily a curated portfolio with graphic and direct storytelling in the feed, featuring mainly in-house produced content such as reels, diagrams, sketches and other visuals. IG [Instagram] Stories and Highlights are used for more flexible and dynamic content with an editorial design grid. These can support pre-planned feed projects or be improvised content as a news output during the week, with both options also aimed at redirecting traffic.'

On LinkedIn, the approach shifts to a mix of visuals and text, making the content more detailed and informative. 'We share our projects with direct links to articles, news, awards and events,

Figure 5.10 Section of Rancho del Bosque, Valle de Bravo, State of Mexico, Mexico, 2024.

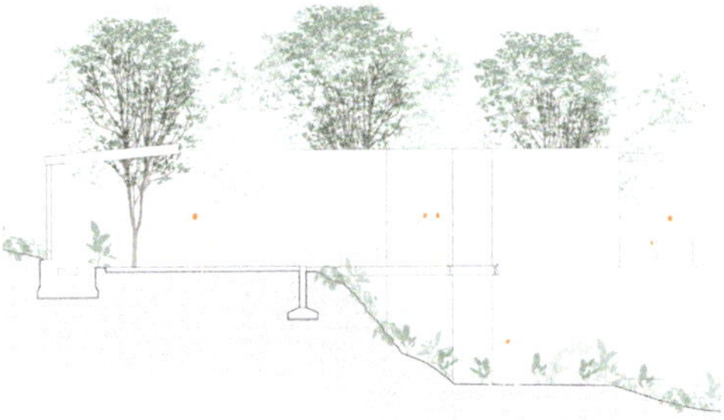

Figure 5.11 Rancho del Bosque, Valle de Bravo, State of Mexico, Mexico, 2024.

and collaborations with employees, institutions and other firms. This content is more readable because there is a better balance between image/video and text. This combination of presenting the same content in different ways on both platforms allows us to nurture our audience while expanding our international reach, especially with the recent opening of our studio in London.'

'Our strategy remains to nurture our local audiences while expanding our global reach. This approach allows us to communicate in both Spanish and English, ensuring the inclusion of diverse audiences. In addition, organic collaborations with international media and related institutions support our social media strategy, allowing us to engage with a wide range of audiences through multiple channels.'

Figure 5.12 Conceptual sketch, SHA Wellness, Cancún, Quintana Roo, Mexico, 2024.

Figure 5.13 Construction process, SHA Wellness, Cancún, Quintana Roo, Mexico, 2024.

Figure 5.14 SHA Wellness, Cancún, Quintana Roo, Mexico, 2024.

Profile Curation

Sordo Madaleno's social media profiles stand out for its curated, professional aesthetic. Every detail reflects its design philosophy and reinforces its 90-year legacy of excellence. Its content – whether photography, sketches, renders or videos – is chosen carefully to convey quality and sophistication.

Its recent rebranding played a crucial role in aligning its communication goals with its visual identity. As explained, 'We maintain a neat visual identity, carefully selecting each image to reflect our design philosophy and the unique storytelling of each project. Our clean branding is meant to let the projects, and their processes, take centre stage.' This thoughtful curation ensures the profiles are not only visually appealing but also a powerful representation of the brand.

Figure 5.15 The Communication Team, Sordo Madaleno, Mexico City, Mexico, 2024.

PROCESS

Sordo Madaleno's approach to content creation is as meticulous as its designs. It involves a wide range of collaborators to craft its content. The process integrates architects, in-house photographers, graphic designers, communicators and digital illustrators to ensure every project's narrative is communicated with depth and precision. This team effort brings together diverse perspectives to capture the essence of the practice's work and its story.

As they describe it, 'The content curation process begins with the selection of key projects in an advanced calendar. Even as the projects are being developed, we communicate with project leaders and design teams to gather existing information. We interview them to identify the central message of each project and discuss the stories, challenges and design solutions that brought the project to life. We then structure these ideas

Figure 5.16 Daily life, London studio, 2024.

Figure 5.17 Daily life, Mexico City office, 2024.

into a cohesive written and graphic narrative. We find it very helpful to have architects involved but also other disciplines in the development of the final message to ensure that it is communicated with the sensitivity necessary to reach architects and non-architects alike. In addition, having a talented in-house team ensures attention to detail, alignment with our values, and time efficiency.'

It's also important to mention that the Fundación Sordo Madaleno (@fundacionsordomadaleno on Instagram) is involved in this documentation process. The Foundation has a variety of social and educational components, one of which is the care of the firm's archive, which preserves and disseminates the 'historical archive' of the firm and keeps up with the continuous compilation of recent and ongoing work generated by the firm. It is called the 'living archive' and includes printed, paper and digital documents.

Figure 5.18 Fundación Sordo Madaleno, archive research, Mexico City, Mexico, 2024.

Figure 5.19 Fundación Sordo Madaleno, historical archive documentation, Mexico City, Mexico, 2024.

Sordo Madaleno exemplifies how a long-established practice can use social media to communicate its design philosophy, share its process and maintain a strong brand identity across multiple platforms. Its transparent, curated approach has helped build trust and expand its global presence while staying true to its architectural values.

An alternative example is Heatherwick Studio who leans into an experimental and dynamic approach to social media. With a strong emphasis on storytelling, human connection and creative risk-taking, the studio implements a strategy to create conversations, spark curiosity and highlight the social impact of its work.

Heatherwick studio

HEATHERWICK STUDIO

Heatherwick Studio designs buildings, public spaces, objects and infrastructure around the world. Completed projects include Little Island in New York, Zeitz MOCAA in Cape Town, Azabudai Hills in Tokyo, and Coal Drops Yard in London.

SOCIAL PLATFORMS

- INSTAGRAM
  @officialheatherwickstudio
- LINKEDIN
  Heatherwick Studio
- YOUTUBE
  Heatherwick Studio
- WECHAT
- REDNOTE
- PINTEREST

CONTENT TYPES

- Short-form video (10–60 seconds)
- Long-form video (1–5 minutes)
- Image – carousels

MESSAGE

Thomas Heatherwick, renowned for his inventiveness and human-centred designs, founded Heatherwick Studio in 1994. The studio offers solutions across architecture, urban planning, product design and interiors, all driven by a desire to create spaces that inspire joy and connection. 'We want to see a world where the buildings and places around us are radically more joyful, engaging and human. As part of this, our team of architects, designers, makers, landscape architects and campaigners share a motivation to design soulful and impactful projects,' the studio explains. Heatherwick Studio's work challenges conventional design norms, focusing on creating environments that engage people emotionally and meaningfully impact individuals' daily lives.

Despite Thomas Heatherwick's global profile and Heatherwick Studio's celebrated portfolio, their journey on social media began relatively recently compared to their peers. As they put it, 'While we have had a LinkedIn presence for a while, we only joined Instagram in 2020 when we decided that in order to campaign for a radically more human world, we needed to start revealing more about our own values and creative process, rather than simply letting our projects speak for themselves as we had always previously done.

'Now, our social media channels manifest our soulful and impactful architectural thinking. They are places where we can share our work, explain our creative process and introduce audiences to some of the 250 people in the studio. For anyone passionate about design or creativity, we hope to inspire and encourage them to think about our towns and cities differently. But perhaps most importantly for us, as designers of public buildings and spaces, it has allowed us to talk about the impact design can have on the world around us.'

STRATEGY

Documenting Their People

While Thomas Heatherwick is a globally recognised figure, social media allows the studio to delve into the creativity of the 250 studio members who work alongside him. It embraces social media as a tool to tell the stories of the people who work there and the people who experience their designs as the end users.

Figure 5.20 Studio founder Thomas Heatherwick.

The studio explains: 'Rather than just sharing beautiful visuals, we want to dig deeper and discuss our projects' social impact. That means we try to share authentic external voices – for example, the people who live, work or spend time in the places we have designed. We also always try to ensure our posts are accessible and our tone of voice is approachable. While we take our work very seriously, we try not to take ourselves too seriously, so there's always space for something playful, fun or curious.'

This content strategy reflects the studio ethos and creates a valuable feedback loop. By documenting the experiences of end users and those involved in the design process, feedback is gathered to help the studio understand what works well and can be improved, directly informing its future designs and ensuring it continues to positively change users' daily lives.

Figure 5.21 Studio members visit the Glasshouse, Woolbeding, West Sussex.

Figure 5.22 A portrait of a resident moving into a Heatherwick building.

Documenting these external voices and sharing them online also helps engage a broad audience interested in the studio's designs or eager to experience its architecture. This accessibility makes it easier to gather diverse perspectives, strengthening its ability to refine and validate its work and encourage people to use its spaces.

Content Variety and Platform Diversification

To share Heatherwick Studio's message, it values each content platform's unique storytelling opportunities and has developed a tailored strategy to make the most of them. It effectively targets and engages different audiences by adapting and packaging its content to suit each platform's strengths. As the studio explains: 'We try to make sure our content is as varied as possible, both in form and content, to communicate engagingly. We post everything from photography and films to infographics, animations, cartoons, drawings, sketches, making tutorials and audio.

Figure 5.23 Widening perspectives in design and construction.

Figure 5.24 A design team at work.

'Not everything appears everywhere – we have different platforms (Instagram, LinkedIn, YouTube, WeChat, RedNote and Pinterest) for various audiences – but we have found a successful approach: publishing on all of them a few times per week. High-quality organic content is our driver of engagement rather than paid-for posts.

'Since adopting social media more meaningfully in 2020, we have added more social channels and seen engagement grow dramatically. We now have audiences worldwide in countries where previously we were perhaps not so well known (such as Japan and South Korea). This has allowed us to engage in a more global conversation about how cities everywhere can be more joyful and engaging. We have been able to convey invention – by showcasing projects like our rolling bridge in Paddington or our dramatically expanding Friction Table – but also demonstrate impact, be it social (our Little Island project) or environmental (our LEED Platinum certified buildings for Google in California).'

Figure 5.25 The studio's creative education workshop.

Figure 5.26 London Olympia – render.

Figure 5.27 London Olympia – reality (construction update).

Figure 5.28 London Olympia Theatre – render.

Figure 5.29 London Olympia Theatre – reality (construction update).

Creative Risk-Taking

Heatherwick Studio is also willing to take creative risks, which is critical to exploring new territories and audiences across social media. The fast-paced world of social media is constantly evolving. Trends emerge, things go viral and topics gain traction every second. Embracing creative risks allows you to break away from your usual content plan and tap into what's popular and relevant. The studio explains: 'We are also always prepared to act quickly to respond to breaking news, project announcements, award wins or media coverage, and we try to keep our posts topical by leading with an issue or theme that we find interesting or important at a given time.

'There are some content formulas that our metrics tell us to perform particularly well – such as major construction updates or anything about new projects – but we are also prepared to take more unconventional creative risks when we have an idea that we think is worth putting out into the world. For example, a video diary captured by our Immersive Media Specialist, Silvia

Figure 5.30 'A Tale of Two Glasshouses: Silvia's Cycling Adventure'.

– a keen cyclist – as she rode her bike for 40 miles between two of our glasshouse projects (Woolbeding in West Sussex and the Bombay Sapphire Distillery in Hampshire) proved so popular it became a recurring mini-series, while one of our earliest posts to make a big audience impression was an Instagram reel of people's cats and dogs sitting in the studio's Spun chairs.'

PROCESS

Heatherwick Studio emphasises that its content production is a collaborative process. It explains that it has built a content team where tasks are allocated and discussed as a team. Collaboration is the cornerstone of everything it does and the production process looks something like this:

1. The Digital Content Curator leads content production, but many people from different teams contribute.
2. A small team makes creative decisions in a weekly content meeting, where ideas are shared and external posts are

Figure 5.31 'A Tale of Two Glasshouses: Silvia's Cycling Adventure'.

reviewed to ensure they tell a compelling story (for example, a group salsa dancing session at Coal Drops Yard in London or an opera performance at Little Island).

3. The Digital Content Curator manages the editorial schedule and works with the Head of Content and Engagement to ensure we reach our audiences – the public, clients and people working in the industry.

'We're fortunate that strong ideas and interest in our social media come from all quarters of the studio, and we have access to amazingly talented designers and filmmakers and an in-house photographer who captures our buildings and studio events. We also have incredible physical and digital archives, so there is never a shortage of content.'

Figure 5.32 The studio has a dedicated Content and Engagement Team.

Figure 5.33 A small team makes creative decisions in a weekly content meeting.

PROFILE SPOTLIGHT

JOHN PAWSON – INSTAGRAM

John Pawson is a renowned British architectural designer celebrated for his minimalist approach to design and attention to detail. His work spans homes, galleries, stores and monasteries. He focuses on light, space and proportion to create calming, beautifully restrained environments. The John Pawson Instagram page effectively reflects this ethos, embracing simplicity and emotion through powerful photography.

Photography is the only content type on the page and has intentional simplicity through the following content features:

+ Close-ups capture intimate moments, focusing on textures, lighting, thresholds and intricate details. These images go beyond mere visual representation – they evoke feelings and emotions, almost inviting you to step into the space.
+ Recognisable and authentic additions, such as a dog or food, add a personal touch to the images. These elements humanise the photos, making them feel more relatable and giving them a point of view.
+ One of the most powerful aspects of the Instagram profile is the absence of captions. The photography quality and story speak for themselves, allowing viewers to interpret and feel them in their own way. This simplicity creates a more personal and emotional experience, as viewers can connect with the imagery without being given any image description or being guided by texts.

This is a powerful example of slicing through the social media noise by decluttering and providing real simplicity. It is a practice precedent of how carefully framed and curated architecture photography can tell a story without any words.

BE PERSONABLE

People are the common denominator of most top architecture social media profiles. We are all nosy. We are all fascinated by what people do and how they do it. We are human; people connect with people, not products.

To take this point to a macro scale, the practices with the largest social media audiences, such as Zaha Hadid Architects (ZHA), Foster + Partners, Heatherwick Studio, BIG and Daniel Libeskind, are celebrated for their groundbreaking designs, but an equally important aspect of their success is how they are associated with the personalities behind them. The architects – Zaha Hadid, Thomas Heatherwick, Bjarke Ingels, Louis Kahn, Le Corbusier and others – have become household names, building personal brands as famous as their work. Why? Because these architects don't just focus on architecture; they actively built a public-facing image. They have held talks, given interviews, written books and participated in high-profile events. This constant public engagement didn't just promote their practice; it humanised them. It made their stories, values and visions accessible to a broader audience, allowing people to connect with their buildings and the architects themselves.

When you see a Zaha Hadid building, you immediately recognise her deconstructivist style. Still, you also associate it with the person – her story, radical design philosophy and brand. ZHA, for instance, has over 1.5 million Instagram followers, a testament to how its strong branding and marketing has extended its reach beyond just the architectural community. Its presence isn't just about showcasing buildings; it's about telling a story and creating an identity with which people want to connect and be associated with.

At a micro scale, architects, designers and solo practitioners such as Gemma Wheeler, Tim Fu, Mariana Cabugueira and Ross Hartland, to name a few, have implemented a strategy focused on unveiling the curtain to the personal side of design and have found great success. Many of these profiles engage with collaborators, attend events, hold talks and engage with their audience either online or in person, which has assisted them in gaining trust and loyalty with their audience. The dedicated personal branding chapter (see Chapter 1: Building a Personal Brand) highlights the decisive role that authenticity, storytelling, brand recognition, USPs and niching play in helping individuals and groups build an audience that truly connects with their brand identity and message.

Mariana Cabugueira, founder of Mariana Cabugueira Studios, affirms the importance of the personal side of social media and believes that the traditional business-to-business (B2B) selling model is fading. Instead, businesses now prefer genuine human connections. 'We want to buy through a human pitch, and if there's a story, even a subtle one, we're hooked,' she says. Mariana's method of showing her business's 'human backstage' – who we are, which is not so different from you – has proven effective. 'Uniqueness is the first step to success,' she says.

For architecture practices, one powerful approach is to embrace personal branding by encouraging individual team members to share their work and experiences online. As Chris Simmons suggests, 'Practices should give their staff autonomy to post about themselves, their process and the work they are involved in; this allows people to build their own online authority whilst promoting the work of the practice to their own network.' This strategy extends social media beyond the practice's official profile. By empowering employees to showcase their expertise and involvement in projects, practices can organically expand their reach, strengthen their brand and foster a sense of shared ownership. Encouraging staff to develop personal networks and upskill in branding, digital communication and content creation benefits both the individual and the practice as a collective. It enhances visibility, attracts talent and clients, and positions the practice as an industry leader – all while cultivating a more engaged and dynamic online presence. This is one way of many ways of looking at it.

As Austin Kleon aptly states, 'Human beings are interested in other human beings and what other human beings do.' This insight is fundamental to building a successful social media profile – people connect with stories, personalities and processes, not just finished projects.

This chapter underscores the transformative potential of social media for architecture practices. By embracing authenticity, storytelling and strategic content creation, practices can move beyond merely showcasing finished projects. Social media offers an unprecedented, accessible platform to engage audiences, build connections and communicate values, helping practices differentiate themselves and foster meaningful professional relationships.

A CONVERSATION WITH
OLIVER THOMAS ARCHI-TECH NETWORK

Oliver Thomas is the founder of Archi-Tech Network (ATN), an online platform to share knowledge at the intersection of architecture and technology in the AEC industry.

In this conversation with Olly Thomas, we delve into the origins of ATN and its mission to bridge the gap between architecture education and practice, particularly in technology adoption.

Thomas: *Why did you decide to position ATN as an educational platform bridging the gap between architecture education and practice, with a focus on technology? What inspired this approach, and how do you aim to help future, current and experienced architects upskill and adapt in this evolving space?*

Olly: ATN emerged from my experience in practice, including working at renowned firms like BIG, where I noticed a significant gap in technology adoption. Young designers, even seniors, often lacked essential tech skills like Rhino, Revit and Grasshopper. When I asked incoming students if they were taught these tools, the basics, the answer was usually no – they were expected to learn from YouTube or received minimal instruction from the university. One of ATN's early content features, 'Project Programmes', highlighted the software firms' use, debunking myths taught at universities. Tutors often promote niche or outdated tools disconnected from real practice.

This disconnect between education and practice struck me as critical. Students pay thousands for education, yet aren't equipped with the necessary tools. Instead, they're either taught outdated software or niche experimental tools. Meanwhile, the industry lags in tech adoption; some firms still debate using Revit, which, while imperfect, is a massive step up from CAD and let's not forget Revit is 20 years old at this point!

ATN started as a way to bridge this gap. When I began teaching online, I realised I was in a unique position – not part of the super-young TikTok crowd nor a typical senior professional. Creating online content at this stage in my career felt unconventional, but I saw an opportunity to bridge a gap. Teaching online became the most efficient way to reach thousands versus a handful of students in a classroom. I also saw an educational gap online – the content was either too basic or dull or taught by people with little to no experience. My experience in practice allowed me to offer practical, engaging insights that weren't widely available online. This inspired me to build ATN as a platform blending professional expertise with accessible teaching, empowering architects with real-world skills in a way that resonated across all levels.

Thomas: *Why do you think it's important to use a variety of content – such as podcasts, office tours and online courses – to give insight into real-world practice? What made you lean into interviews with industry professionals and explore office spaces to showcase tools, processes and people shaping architecture today?*

Olly: ATN focuses on technology in practice because it's less guarded than design processes. While firms like BIG, Foster + Partners or Zaha Hadid Architects (ZHA) keep their design methods proprietary, technology tools like Rhino, Revit and Grasshopper are universal, with everyone facing similar challenges. Unlike designers who compete directly, technology professionals across offices often share insights, creating a collaborative environment.

We experimented with different forms of knowledge-sharing. We started simply as a podcast on Clubhouse, which we now continue on YouTube, but we also started introducing other video content like the tours; we also hosted in-person events called Pecha Kucha in the pub. Our core educational format is our 'masterclasses' courses, where we get the best tutors we can find to teach real-world technology you actually need in practice.

The office tours grew from this same ethos – revealing the culture, philosophy and technology behind top firms. Our goal is to unveil the curtain a little bit behind these firms. Visiting offices like ZHA and Heatherwick Studio during my consulting days showed how uniquely each firm operates. These tours, now part of ATN's content, spotlight technology professionals who often remain behind the scenes, offering insights into the fundamental processes driving architectural innovation. Do I try to engineer how a firm looks in my content? No, it's not engineered. The character of the practice naturally shines through – it reflects its unique culture, design philosophy and approach. My role is to showcase that authenticity rather than curate or manipulate it into something it's not.

Thomas: *What's your take on practices encouraging their team to post online and connect through social media? Do you think it benefits both individuals and firms? And what advice would you give to someone in practice who's just starting their social media journey?*

Olly: I was fortunate to work at BIG, where the culture is progressive and open to sharing ideas. At BIG, there's even encouragement for employees to represent the firm publicly, which aligns perfectly with my journey in creating ATN. Not every firm is this open, and it would have been harder to build ATN in a more restrictive environment.

For those looking to build a personal brand while working in practice, my advice is to go for it but be strategic and respectful absolutely. Establish yourself within the firm first – build trust and credibility before promoting your brand. Starting on day one with a vlog or 'day in the life' featuring confidential projects can rub colleagues the wrong way, harm your reputation and potentially cause legal issues. Instead, involve your practice in your plans, where appropriate, and maintain clear boundaries if the firm is less supportive.

For architecture practices, platforms like YouTube remain an untapped resource. Firms could benefit significantly from storytelling – offering behind-the-scenes looks at projects or documenting the design process. Creators like Dami Lee have successfully educated audiences on architecture, but few focus on how projects come to life. With the right approach, firms could transform storytelling into a powerful tool for engagement.

CHECKLIST: FIVE MANAGEABLE STEPS TO START CREATING CONTENT TODAY

1. DEFINE YOUR MESSAGE

Defining your 'message' is the most critical first step in building a social media profile because it establishes the foundation for building the brand. This message should encapsulate the brand identity and story you want to tell through your brand. It will guide and dictate your brand, content and marketing strategy. Your message and identity will differentiate your brand from the others in a competitive marketplace.

You must understand your brand's core values and unique attributes to define your message effectively. This involves identifying what your brand stands for, its mission and vision, and the problems it seeks to solve for its audience.

Ask yourself these questions:

+ What story do I want to tell?
+ What identity do I want to create?
+ What about my message is unique?
+ What am I offering that is different from other brands?
+ How could I communicate that message?

Building an identity helps to streamline and clarify your message. Clarity is fundamental. No one will listen to your message if it isn't clear. The human brain is drawn to clarity, not confusion.[1]

SIMPLICITY, CREATIVITY AND INDIVIDUALITY

Each profile highlighted in the book has a clear identity, with a defined message that anchors its content and consistently repeats throughout its profile. I liken this to how you define a concept for an architecture project – it sets the foundation for every design decision and direction you take. The concept is the anchor, and the project should always refer back to it.

The same applies here. The importance of a clear message is evident at all scales of business. Major brands like Apple, Nike and Coca-Cola have strong, identifiable messages.

+ **Apple is an excellent example of this.** Its message focuses on simplicity, creativity and individuality. From product design to ads, Apple emphasises making technology easy to use while empowering creativity and celebrating uniqueness. This was perfectly captured in the 'Think Different' campaign, portraying Apple as a company driving change and innovation for those who see the world differently.
+ **Nike's message is just as precise.** 'Just Do It' inspires athletes at every level to push themselves and chase their goals. This idea of perseverance runs through their campaigns, athlete partnerships and products.
+ **Coca-Cola centres its message on happiness, sharing and togetherness.** It often showcases moments of joy and connection in its ads, reinforcing that Coca-Cola brings people together.

These clear messages from Apple, Nike and Coca-Cola have built loyal customer bases that connect with their values, helping these brands become globally recognised.

2. BUILD A STRATEGY

Once the message is defined, it drives the brand and content strategy. Every content, be it a social media post, advertisement, blog or podcast episode, should reflect and reinforce the brand message. This alignment ensures that the brand consistently communicates its values and develops brand recognition.

The strategy is the planned brand, content and marketing scheme. It is a long-term plan for achieving the objectives outlined for your brand.

The process of building a strategy involves:

1. Define clear objectives
2. Select your target market
3. Choose a content type/s
4. Choose your social platform/s
5. Build a content strategy.

DEFINE CLEAR OBJECTIVES

First and foremost, you must outline your brand's objectives. Objectives serve as a roadmap, guiding the social media and marketing strategy toward achieving specific goals. Identify what you want to accomplish with your content. Objectives could include:

+ increasing brand awareness
+ driving website traffic
+ boosting sales of a product
+ documentation
+ building an email database.

You may decide to target one objective or multiple objectives. These will instruct the strategy and provide direction and purpose, helping to align the content strategy with the brand's mission.

SELECT YOUR TARGET MARKET

Selecting your target market is critical. To increase brand awareness, drive website traffic or build an email database, you must target an audience that demands your content. Start by thinking of common problems your content can solve. Identify a problem and offer a solution.

Channel demand with these steps:

a. Position yourself as a viewer

Positioning yourself as the viewer helps you understand your target market's needs and demands by allowing you to see through their eyes.

b. Create an avatar

Creating an avatar is powerful for identifying the exact needs and situation of a character. For example:

Susan, a 37-year-old maths teacher looking on Instagram for fast and low-budget cooking recipes to feed her children after work, isn't interested in your step-by-step content for creating animated exploded axonometrics.

Conversely, Adam, a 23-year-old, third-year architecture student with a portfolio submission approaching, who needs to create drawings to sell his project, may be much more likely to engage with your brand and content.

c. Find pain points

Finding points of pain is crucial for discovering a demand. It identifies audiences seeking solutions to their problems, ensuring your content addresses real-life issues.

CHOOSE A CONTENT TYPE/S

Selecting the appropriate content form is crucial to effectively engage with your target audience. Different content forms – short-form videos, static posts, podcasts, long-form videos and blog posts – cater to varied audience needs and consumption patterns.

Video content is popular because it offers a multi-sensory experience combining visuals, audio and text, making it inherently compelling and memorable. The dynamic nature of video allows individuals/groups to convey complex messages, tell stories and evoke emotions concisely and impactfully. This is particularly true of architecture, which is intrinsically visual, relying on drawings, imagery, physical models and buildings to communicate ideas, space and experience.

To choose the most effective content form, consider your audience's lifestyle, preferences and the platform they use. Analyse your target demographic and respond to the questions created in your avatar:

+ Are they busy professionals?
+ Are they avid learners?
+ Are they visual explorers?

Align your content strategy with their consumption habits. For instance, a tech brand might use blogs and long-form videos for tech enthusiasts, while a lifestyle brand might focus on short-form videos and static posts for quick, engaging updates. By understanding your audience's needs, you can select the right mix of content forms to maximise engagement and reach.

CHOOSE YOUR SOCIAL PLATFORM/S

Once you have chosen the content type that best communicates your message, selecting the right social media platform is critical. Different platforms favour various content types, algorithms and demographics, impacting your reach and engagement with your target audience. Choose wisely.

BUILD A CONTENT STRATEGY

Once you've defined clear objectives, identified your target market, chosen your content type/s and selected social media platforms, the next step is to craft a strategy that makes your brand and content approach unique.

To stand out among competitors, consider the following strategies:

1. Authenticity
2. Niching
3. Defining a unique selling proposition (USP)
4. Utilising storytelling
5. Building brand recognition.

These strategies will help you communicate your brand message clearly and engagingly, reaching a global audience. Choose multiple strategies to layer your brand strategy and maximise your potential of being seen and remembered.

3. PRODUCE CONTENT

Once you have defined your message and strategised your social media approach, the next stage is to outline your production process for creating content. The production level will vary, based on your strategy and the look and feel you want to achieve. The production process will also refer to your initial outline of brand objectives.

Time, budget, resources and desired production quality will influence your process. Consider questions like:

+ How much time can you dedicate to content creation?
+ What is your budget for equipment and software?
+ Do you have the necessary skills and personnel to produce high-quality content?
+ What level of production quality is required to achieve the desired objectives?

Addressing these questions will help shape a production process that aligns with your objectives and capabilities.

EXAMPLES OF CONTENT PRODUCTION

1. Architecture practice example

If you aim to showcase completed projects through photography and videography, high-production quality is essential to capture the details, materiality, context and design quality. This example approach may require investing in camera equipment and professional editing software to ensure the visuals are compelling and accurately represent your work.

2. Personal brand example

A more accessible and intimate production process is suitable for building a brand around authentically documenting your journey. Filming on a phone or a point-and-shoot vlogging camera, like the Canon G7 X Mark II, allows you to create relatable content that resonates with your audience without needing high-end equipment.

3. High-quality podcast

Producing a high-quality visual and audio podcast demands a professional set-up. You may need a podcast studio with good lighting, camera set-ups, a team to handle the cameras, editors and sound engineers. This set-up ensures that the audio and visual elements are polished and engaging for your audience.

Example of a production workflow:

1. **Ideation:** Generate and brainstorm content ideas that align with your strategy and goals.
2. **Scripting/structuring:** Develop scripts or outlines to organise your content to communicate your message.
3. **Filming:** Capture the necessary footage or audio using the appropriate equipment.
4. **Editing/post-production:** Edit the content to enhance quality and convey the intended message.
5. **Scheduling:** Plan the timing and platform for publishing the content to maximise reach and engagement.
6. **Publishing:** Release the content on your chosen social media platforms and monitor its performance to inform future content strategies.

4. FIND CONSISTENCY

Every social media profile highlighted in this book didn't achieve success overnight. Building a strong social media presence and a solid content creation strategy takes time. It's a journey with ups and downs; sometimes, you might feel stuck or that you are not making progress. This is normal. Consistency and adaptability are key to navigating these moments and growing your brand. Social media can be unpredictable – what works one day might not work the next. Algorithms change, trends shift and audience preferences evolve. It's important not to get discouraged when things seem stagnant or a post doesn't perform as expected. These bad days are part of the journey. The key is to weather the storms and continue delivering value to your audience, even when the results aren't immediate.

BRAND AND CONTENT CONSISTENCY

Each post and every action you take is an opportunity to engage with new followers and give someone a reason to connect with your brand. Think of your social media presence as a fire. Each piece of content is like a log you add to the fire to keep it burning. If you stop adding fuel, the fire will go out. The same applies to your social media efforts – consistent posting keeps your brand alive and growing. Creating a content schedule is one of the best ways to stay consistent. Set realistic goals for how often you can post, and stick to them.

Brand consistency maintains a unified message, look and experience across all platforms to form a clear brand identity. It ensures that every interaction with your audience reinforces who you are and what your brand stands for. Consistent messaging helps repeatedly communicate your core values and message, strengthening your brand's presence. A unified look and feel – through colour schemes, video style and design – make your brand visually recognisable. Lastly, offering a consistent experience across all touchpoints builds trust and reliability, ensuring your audience knows what to expect and making your brand more memorable and trusted.

Consistency not only helps reinforce your message, but also builds recognition over time. People are busy, and social media is fast-paced. It takes time for your brand to stick in someone's mind, but posting regularly with discipline ensures your message remains visible.

5. START NOW

A quote from Alex Hormozi resonates deeply: 'The best day to start your business was the day you were born, the second best day is today.'[2] It's a powerful reminder that while we can't go back and start sooner, we always have the opportunity to begin right now.

Whether that step is downloading LinkedIn, setting up your account, making your first connection, releasing that video you've been hesitant to share or recording yourself for the first time – today is the day to start. Maybe it's about investing more time and resources into social media, being more transparent in your content or stepping into a new social platform; whatever your starting point, now is the time. Every journey begins with the first step, and today is the perfect time to take yours.

Leaping into social media is a nerve-racking step requiring a level of vulnerability and unveiling who you are and what you do. To take the leap rather than viewing vulnerability and transparency as an on-and-off switch, take it as a dial that you can turn up and down. You don't need to reveal everything. First, take small nuggets of lessons learned, experiences and knowledge associated with your brand message.

TEST, FAIL AND LEARN

You will fail numerous times and will sometimes feel like you are wasting your time. Part of finding success, whatever success looks to you, will happen from learning from failures or mistakes. Not every post will be a hit. 95% of your posts, especially initially, may not see significant engagement or growth. That's okay. The key is to keep experimenting, trying new things and paying attention to your audience's response. When you find that 5% of content resonates with your community, double down on it, and this will help build momentum. This you must monitor closely.

It is crucial to listen to your audience and monitor how they respond to your content. You can do this by tracking analytics and studying the numbers. Still, a more significant barometer of success lies in the comment section – engaging with your audience by asking them questions and hearing their opinions. Once you build an audience and find methods to engage them, keep things fresh and change things up. Test new content methods and continue to communicate your message.

Your message is the foundation of everything you build. It shapes your brand, content and strategy, defining how you connect with your audience. The message alone isn't enough – clarity, consistency and action are key.

Start today with the Architectural Influence Framework. Put your message to the people who need it, refine it and adapt. Success isn't instant, but persistence pays off. Test, learn and grow. Whether you're an individual or a practice, social media is an open stage – step forward, take control and make your impact.

BIBLIOGRAPHY

BOOKS

Dib, A. *The 1-Page Marketing Plan: Get New Customers, Make More Money, and Stand Out From the Crowd*, Vancouver, Page Two, 2018

Hormozi, A. *$100M Leads: How to Get Strangers To Want To Buy Your Stuff*, Acquisition.com, 2023

Kleon, A. *Show Your Work! 10 Ways To Share Your Creativity And Get Discovered*, New York, Workman Publishing, 2014

Miller, D. *Building a Storybrand: Clarify Your Message So Customers Will Listen*, Nashville, HarperCollins Leadership, 2017

Walker, D. *The 90 Day Brand Plan: How to Unleash Your Personal Brand to Dominate the Competition and Scale Your Business*, New Jersey, Wiley 2024

WEBSITES

Architecture Candy, 'Home' [website], https://thearchitecturecandy.com/ (accessed 10 September 2024)

BT Group Newsroom, 'Social media is now the top sales generator for one in four UK small businesses', 2023, https://newsroom.bt.com/social-media-is-now-the-top-sales-generator-for-one-in-four-uk-small-businesses/ (accessed 24 September 2024)

J. Gamolina, 'Through the Lens of Architecture: Architect and YouTuber Dami Lee on Content Creation, Leadership, and Self-Acceptance', *Madame Architect*, 2023, https://www.madamearchitect.org/interviews/2023/8/24/dami-lee (accessed 10 September 2024)

'Influencer Marketing Benchmark Report 2025', *Influencer Marketing Hub*, 2025 https://influencermarketinghub.com/influencer-marketing-benchmark-report/ (accessed 22 February 2025)

News Release, 'ARB announces fundamental reforms to architectural education', *Architects Registration Board*, 2021, https://arb.org.uk/arb-announces-fundamental-reforms-to-architectural-education-2/ (accessed 4 February 2025)

Sears, E., 'Marketing for Architects: The Authoritative Guide (with Examples)', *Business of Architecture*, 2017, https://www.businessofarchitecture.com/marketing-for-architects/ (accessed 10 September 2024)

Show it Better, Courses for Architects [website], https://www.showitbetter.co/courses/ (accessed 9 September 2024)

'The 2024 Future of the Creator Economy Report is out now!', *Epidemic Sound*, 2024, https://www.epidemicsound.com/blog/the-future-of-the-creator-economy-report-2024/#:~:text=Creators%20remain%20optimistic%20about%20income,the%2071%25%20reported%20in%202023 (accessed 9 September 2024)

30X40, 'About' [website], https://thirtybyforty.com/about (accessed 16 February 2025)

Waite, R., 'Which architecture practice is the most popular on social media?', *Architects' Journal*, 2024, https://www.architectsjournal.co.uk/news/which-architecture-practice-is-the-most-popular-on-social-media (accessed 3 February 2025)

Wong, B., 'Top Social Media Statistics And Trends of 2024', *Forbes*, 2023, https://www.forbes.com/advisor/business/social-media-statistics/ (accessed 22 September 2024)

Zimmerman, B., 'The Importance Of Authenticity And Loyalty In Brand Partnerships', *Forbes*, 2022, https://www.forbes.com/councils/theyec/2022/05/04/the-importance-of-authenticity-and-loyalty-in-brand-partnerships/ (accessed 8 September 2024)

YOUTUBE

How this Architect 4X'd His Income' 30X40 Design Workshop, 2025, https://www.youtube.com/watch?v=gZIx2aUDTC4&t=569s (accessed 20 February 2025)

REFERENCES

AN INTRODUCTION TO ARCHITECTURE CONTENT CREATION

1 B. Wong, 'Top Social Media Statistics And Trends of 2024', *Forbes*, 2023, https://www.forbes.com/advisor/business/social-media-statistics/ (accessed 22 September 2024).

2 R. Waite, 'Which architecture practice is the most popular on social media?', *Architects' Journal*, 2024, https://www.architectsjournal.co.uk/news/which-architecture-practice-is-the-most-popular-on-social-media (accessed 3 February 2025).

3 News Release, 'ARB announces fundamental reforms to architectural education', *Architects Registration Board*, 2021, https://arb.org.uk/arb-announces-fundamental-reforms-to-architectural-education-2/ (accessed 4 February 2025).

4 B. Wong, 'Top Social Media Statistics And Trends of 2024', *Forbes*, 2023, https://www.forbes.com/advisor/business/social-media-statistics/ (accessed 22 September 2024).

5 BT Group Newsroom, 'Social media is now the top sales generator for one in four UK small businesses', 2023, https://newsroom.bt.com/social-media-is-now-the-top-sales-generator-for-one-in-four-uk-small-businesses/ (accessed 24 September 2024).

CHAPTER 1

1 A. Kleon, *Show Your Work! 10 Ways To Share Your Creativity And Get Discovered*, New York, Workman Publishing, 2014, p 95.

2 A. Dib, *The 1-Page Marketing Plan: Get New Customers, Make More Money, and Stand Out From the Crowd*, Vancouver, Page Two, 2018, p 51.

3 *Ibid.*, p 34.

CHAPTER 3

1 J. Gamolina, 'Through the Lens of Architecture: Architect and YouTuber Dami Lee on Content Creation, Leadership, and Self-Acceptance', *Madame Architect*, 2023, https://www.madamearchitect.org/interviews/2023/8/24/dami-lee (accessed 10 September 2024).

CHAPTER 4

1 A. Kleon, *Show Your Work! 10 Ways To Share Your Creativity And Get Discovered*, New York, Workman Publishing, 2014, p 161.

2 E. Sears, 'Marketing for Architects: The Authoritative Guide (with Examples)', *Business of Architecture*, 2017, https://www.businessofarchitecture.com/marketing-for-architects/ (accessed 10 September 2024).

3 *Ibid.*

4 Show it Better, Courses for Architects [website], https://www.showitbetter.co/courses/ (accessed 9 September 2024).

5 Architecture Candy, Home [website], https://thearchitecturecandy.com/ (accessed 10 September 2024).

6 A. Hormozi, *$100M Leads: How to Get Strangers To Want To Buy Your Stuff*, Acquisition.com, 2023.

7 *Ibid.*

8 'Influencer Marketing Benchmark Report 2025', *Influencer Marketing Hub*, 2025 https://influencermarketinghub.com/influencer-marketing-benchmark-report/ (accessed 22 February 2025).

9 B. Zimmerman, 'The Importance Of Authenticity And Loyalty In Brand Partnerships', *Forbes*, 2022, https://www.forbes.com/councils/theyec/2022/05/04/the-importance-of-authenticity-and-loyalty-in-brand-partnerships/ (accessed 8 September 2024).

10 'The 2024 Future of the Creator Economy Report is out now!', *Epidemic Sound*, 2024, https://www.epidemicsound.com/blog/the-future-of-the-creator-economy-report-2024/#:~:text=Creators%20remain%20optimistic%20about%20income,the%2071%25%20reported%20in%202023 (accessed 9 September 2024).

CHAPTER 5

1 'How this Architect 4X'd His Income' 30X40 Design Workshop, 2025, https://www.youtube.com/watch?v=gZIx2aUDTC4&t=569s (accessed 20 February 2025).

2 *Ibid.*

3 *Ibid.*

CHECKLIST: FIVE MANAGEABLE STEPS TO START CREATING CONTENT TODAY

1 D. Miller, *Building a StoryBrand: Clarify Your Message So Customers Will Listen*, Nashville, HarperCollins Leadership, 2017.

2 A. Hormozi, *$100M Leads: How to Get Strangers To Want To Buy Your Stuff*, Acquisition.com, 2023

INDEX

IMAGE CREDITS

IV, 51; Fig 1.35–1.48, 4.12–4.15 **Thomas Rowntree**

17 **Satwinder Samra**

25; Fig 1.1, 1.3–1.12 **Abby. Architecture**

Fig 1.2 **Ryan Sarakul**

34; Fig 1.13–1.23, 4.5–4.6, 5.1–5.4 **Initiate Architecture**

42; Fig 1.24–1.34 **Chris Simmons**

65; Fig 1.50–1.51, 1.55, 1.57 **Ana Aragão**

Fig 1.49 **Cláudia Rocha**

Fig 1.52, 1.56, 1.58 **Miguel C. Tavares**

Fig 1.53–1.54 **Cláudia Rocha and Underdogs**

Fig 1.59 **CMP**

74; Fig 1.60–1.67 **Tim Fu**

82 **Mariana Cabugueira**

89; Fig 2.1–2.9, 4.10–4.11 **ArchAdemia**

99; Fig 2.10–2.21, 4.1–4.2 **Show it Better**

107; Fig 2.22–2.35, 4.3–4.4 **Architecture Candy**

115; Fig 2.36–2.47 **The Second Studio**

122; Fig 2.48–2.59 **Blessedarch**

130 **Oliver Uszkurat**

138; Fig 3.1–3.14 **Alvin Zhu**

147; Fig 3.15–3.22 **POoR Collective**

156; Fig 3.23–3.30 **Dami Lee**

Fig 3.31–3.36 **Eric W. Reinholdt**

169 **Noris Obijiaku**

Fig 4.7–4.9; 196 **David Drazil**

211; Fig 5.5–5.6, 5.8–5.10, 5.12, 5.15–5.19 **Sordo Madaleno**

Fig 5.7, 5.14 **Rafael Gamo**

Fig 5.11 **Edmund Sumner**

Fig 5.13 **Óscar Caballero**

221; Fig 5.20–5.33 **Heatherwick Studio**

234 **Oliver Thomas**